Finding the Time for Instructional Leadership

Management Strategies for Strengthening the Academic Program

John C. Leonard

ROWMAN & LITTLEFIELD EDUCATION

A division of
ROWMAN & LITTLEFIELD PUBLISHERS, INC.
Lanham • Boulder • New York • Toronto • Plymouth, UK

ROWMAN & LITTLEFIELD PUBLISHERS, INC.

Published in the United States of America
by Rowman & Littlefield Education
A wholly owned subsidiary of The Rowman & Littlefield Publishing Group, Inc.
4501 Forbes Boulevard, Suite 200, Lanham, Maryland 20706
www.rowmanlittlefield.com

Estover Road
Plymouth PL6 7PY
United Kingdom

British Library Cataloguing in Publication Information Available

Library of Congress Cataloging-in-Publication Data

Leonard, John C.
  Finding the time for instructional leadership : management strategies for
strengthening the academic program / John C. Leonard.
     p. cm.
  Includes bibliographical references.
  ISBN 978-1-60709-614-6 (cloth : alk. paper) — ISBN 978-1-60709-615-3 (pbk. : alk.
paper) — ISBN 978-1-60709-593-4 (electronic)
  1. Educational leadership. 2. School management and organization.
3. Organizational behavior. I. Title.
LB2805.L3864 2010
371.2—dc22   2010016854

Printed in the United States of America

∞ ™ The paper used in this publication meets the minimum requirements of
American National Standard for Information Sciences—Permanence of Paper
for Printed Library Materials, ANSI/NISO Z39.48-1992.

To those dedicated principals who lead with a passion for improving your school one child at a time, I commend your service to our educational system and dedicate this work to you. It is my hope that my grandchildren, McKenna and Jayson, will be the beneficiaries of the school improvement work being done by these outstanding professionals.

Additionally, this book would not have been possible without the mentoring of the many professional educators who have so positively touched my life and I express my enduring gratitude to them for their mentorship.

I would be remiss if I did not recognize my loving family for their support. I am especially blessed to have the love of my wonderful wife, George Ann, who each and every day inspires me to strive to make the world a better place.

~

Contents

~

Illustrations

List of Figures

List of Tables

Preface

Throughout my career as a campus- and district-level administrator, and for the last eight years as an instructor in a principal preparation program, I have had the privilege of visiting with many dedicated principals. When they can slow down enough to visit, I ask them to share the number one challenge they face in the principalship. Perhaps surprising to some, it is not high-stakes testing, No Child Left Behind, student discipline, campus security, paperwork, or providing a high-quality education to every student within limited budgets. Invariably principals respond that they simply cannot find the time to be the instructional leader they know they can, and should, be.

These are dedicated professionals who carry the mantle of instructional leadership and responsibility for providing every student with a high-quality education very seriously. Typically, they are putting in an incredible number of work hours each week, both at their school and with the unfinished work they take home. These individuals are crying out for support and for new ideas that can be utilized to redirect their time and energy to the teaching and learning process. This book targets these campus-level educational leaders and seeks to provide them with sound personal management strategies needed for instructional leadership and for maintaining their sanity as they struggle against the clock to achieve instructional success.

The gap between available time and instructionally engaged time provides the backdrop for investigating ways principals eager to improve the teaching-learning process on their campus can accomplish both the required management-related tasks and, more importantly, find more time redirected toward the support of teachers and for strengthening the school's academic program.

At the core of these ideas is the author's advocacy for campuses to create a Value Added Unified Leadership Team (VAULT). This distributed leadership concept, taken together with the personal management strategies presented in the book, provides a framework for creating a positive campus work environment by freeing up valuable minutes for the VAULT instructional team.

The VAULT strategies focus more on a leader building a team by cultivating the strengths of its members rather than trying to overcome deficient areas of their leadership skills. Cultivating a broad-based, inclusive leadership team distributes the work and serves the ancillary, *value added*, benefits of fostering collaboration and nurturing leadership in others.

This book constructs the case for time challenged principals reassessing where time is currently spent and how the time management strategies found in these pages relate to their practice. Successful VAULT teams can energize their campus's instructional practices and afford a high-quality education for all students and, at the same time, reenergize the school's leadership.

Finding the Time for Instructional Leadership: Management Strategies for Strengthening the Academic Program will provide campus instructional personnel—including principals, associate/assistant principals, campus instructional support personnel, and teacher leaders—with keys for the successful integration of proven time management strategies into the daily accomplishment of the core teaching-learning process. The seven keys explored in the core chapters include

Key #1—Realizing that school leaders are *time challenged* and that conventional approaches to academic leadership produce unrealistic requirements for leaders.

Key #2—Recognizing the reality of time management myths and how to overcome the time traps inherent in each.

Key #3—Admitting that micromanagement is a debilitating leadership addiction and a successful cure is creating a distributive leadership team that positively impacts the success of students.

Key #4—Knowing that collaboration through distributive leadership can lead to improved academic performance through a *Value Added Unified Leadership Team* (VAULT) approach will lead to improved instructional support.

Key #5—Knowing how to facilitate the organization of a VAULT academic improvement collaborative will assist with the structuring of instructional improvement process tasks.

Key #6—Knowing that a motivated self leads to motivated others in the organization will invigorate the school with students becoming the academic beneficiaries.

Key #7—Understanding that reflection is a key to continued renewal of the VAULT.

As these truisms are presented the associated time management strategies will be deconstructed for the reader and reconstructed within a value added distributed leadership approach. Although situated within a campus perspective, the VAULT approach should be considered as being applicable to any organization wanting to tap into its underidentified leadership capital.

Finally, does this book present revolutionary concepts that will prove to be the next great breakthrough in organizational management or offer secrets no one is acquainted with about time management? The answer, of course, is "No!" What this book does is offer busy school leaders some well-measured strategies for finding the instructional leader in themselves. This book's success will be gauged in large part by the amount of instructional leadership time recovered and its impact of student success and equity. The author hopes the concepts reflected in the following chapters will guide your school to *vault* to the next level!

CHAPTER ONE

~

Framing the Issue of Principal Time

Across the country busy principals yearn for the "good old days" when their lives were less challenged by standards, accountability, and a myriad of other forces impacting their day. Truth is, those bygone days were probably not that great but there did seem to be enough time to get all the tasks accomplished and still find time to reflect on our practice. Where does the principal find valuable minutes to accomplish his or her vision and shepherd the school's academic mission?

Few would dispute the fact that twenty-first-century school leaders are finding it difficult to keep up with the pressures brought to bear on their profession. Demands placed on the principal for solving many of society's ills, maintaining safe schools, stretching limited budgets, and countless competing claims on the principal's time all serve to dilute instructional leadership, supervision, and professional development.

Shahid et al. (2001) affirm the struggles faced by principals in describing a typical work day as "filled with a never ending series of reports, phone calls, student discipline problems, parent visits, personnel problems, and requests to make appearances both off and on campus" (506). The inevitable conflict that arises in handling the management-related tasks, as well as leading the school's instructional program, poses a significant dilemma for conscientious principals.

This disconnect between available time and instructionally engaged time provides the backdrop for investigating ways principals desirous of improving the teaching-learning process can accomplish both the management-related tasks and find more time to dedicate to supporting teachers and strengthening the school's academic program. As Sergiovanni (2006) states, "Principals are responsible for helping their schools get smarter. Smarter schools mean more student learning" (269).

The notion of working smarter requires principals to adopt a singular, nonnegotiable mind-set on their campus for, as Covey, Merrill, and Merrill (1994) aptly state, "the main thing is keeping the main thing the main thing" (75). The main thing has to be the improvement of the school's instructional program that results in student success and equity.

This can only be accomplished if principals truly value a teaching-learning environment and understand the vital role they play in accomplishing the school's academic mission. Deal and Peterson (2007) convey the importance of the principal taking the visionary lead for messaging what is important in their school stating, "Everyone watches leaders in a school. Everything they do gets people's attention. Educational philosophy, teaching reputation, demeanor, communication style, and other characteristics are important signals that will be read by members of the culture in a variety of ways" (201). Communicating the importance of instructional issues must flow from the principal's visioning process as represented by significant personal actions that reflect a laser-focus for the continual improvement of the teaching-learning process.

The emphasis on the instructional leadership role for principals is well established in the school improvement literature. Murphy, Elliott, Goldring, and Porter (2007) agree with other scholars on the vital role of instructional leadership and found instructional leadership included "the ability of leaders to (a) stay consistently focused on the right stuff—the core technology of schooling, or learning, teaching, curriculum and assessment and (b) to make all the other dimensions of schooling (e.g., administration, organization, finance) work in the service of a more robust core technology and improved student learning" (179).

What is not so evident in the school improvement literature is how principals overcome the many demands made on their time that serve to detract from their role as leader of instruction and find time to be effective in that realm. Principal time management studies show a stark contrast between the perceptions of how principals should prioritize their time and the reality of their primary role as the chief instructional officer for the campus.

This on-the-job reality poses a significant test for principals as they search for strategies for accomplishing the instructional goals for their campuses. Kelly and Peterson (2007) address this problem stating, "The daily work of principals is little understood and yet extremely complex. The nature of a principal's work suggests the need for schools and districts to consider ways to substantially reframe or restructure it to enable principals to accomplish the tasks expected of them. One approach might restructure the work to enable principals to engage more fully in instructional improvement" (356). For schools to reallocate the work of principals and, thus, refocus their attention toward the preeminence of instructional issues, innovative strategies must be explored.

Conscientious principals cannot afford the luxury of expecting others, whether campus or district staff, to resolve the time constraints they face. Principals desirous of school improvement goal attainment have to proactively search for the means to the desired end. Principals must reflect on the overarching goal for the continuous improvement of the school's instructional program and the significance of their leadership for the accomplishment of these goals.

The value of reflection, as Donaldson and Marnik (1995) report in their work with the Maine Academy for School Leaders (MASL), is a habit needed for principals to make sense of their world, "Members found the newly acquired habit of reflection a mechanism for managing their feelings of being overwhelmed by the demands of leadership. Like school leaders elsewhere, these Maine leaders felt burdened by the physical and emotional exhaustion of running their schools, spearheading a reform, or alleviating negativism and defeatism among colleagues" (132). Thoughtful reflection provides the springboard for analyzing and, thus, finding meaning with school-related issues and for redirecting the leader's energy toward the instructional mission of the school.

Seeking solutions through reflection can lead to a better understanding of the leader's priorities and utilization of the precious commodity of time. This awareness will predictably lead to the truism that the issue of never having enough time to handle all the tasks and responsibilities of the principalship has never been about time, per se. It is the comprehension that time is a fixed commodity that all leaders struggle with as they navigate their personal response to the challenges they face.

What This Book Is About

This book is centered on the principalship and is designed to offer busy school leaders time management strategies for finding the time to be genuine instructional leaders. Readers of this book will find a set of tactics—called keys—that will guide their reflection on the issue of instructional management. These seven keys offer the principal suggestions for overcoming the daily barrage of secondary responsibilities that redirect valuable time and energy away from academics.

The keys offered are not in a prioritized "must do" list nor are they intended to be an "all or none" approach. Principals searching for time solutions are encouraged to consider each of the keys and adopt, adapt, or reject the suggestion as fits their personal leadership circumstances.

Why This Book Is Important

The management of one's own fixed amount of time depends on how well he or she can change personally to accomplish organizational goals. All principals toil within the same twenty-four hours in a day and reasonably similar instructional calendars for their school year. The variable that must be manipulated is the individual and how he or she uses the available time to focus on instruction and still manage the other tasks and responsibilities faced each day.

The target audience for this book are principals who are feeling burned out and are considering leaving the principalship as well as those who are remaining at the helm of their school but feel frustrated by not being able to guide the instructional program as they wish. The intent of this book is to offer more than solace to school leaders by providing research-based, common-sense time control solutions that allow more time directed toward instruction, teacher support, and professional development.

Rather than being a prescriptive time management book, it simply takes up seven loosely connected "keys" that can assist principals in gaining both an understanding of the concept and suggestions for approaches to their practice. The keys are considered within a model of shared instructional responsibility termed the Value Added Unified Leadership Team (VAULT) approach. The essence of the value added aspect is the realized benefits when the principal shares leadership in order to accomplish the school's goals. A win-win school environment is created that capitalizes on the talents and artistry of the Value Added Unified Leadership Team.

The author uses VAULT as a less deep-seated acronym with a twofold meaning to "leap over a barrier" and is used as imagery for overcoming obstacles and striving for greatness. Also attached to the acronym VAULT is a secondary representation as the unlocking of a vault containing the wisdom of reflective shared leadership—a vault of wisdom (*Webster's Dictionary*, 2023). Both the concept of overcoming obstacles and unlocking one's mind are crucial for effective understanding of how personal time management impacts student success, the overarching purpose of this book.

Value Added Unified Leadership Team

Instructional leadership requires the principal to clearly understand that the positional responsibilities are too numerous and too complex for a Lone Ranger approach. Tom Peters (1997) equates the building of leadership capacity in others to the leader's ability to create "Michelangelos" within the organization by collapsing "500 job categories to . . . 1"—his term for decentralizing the organization's work by empowering others (131). Cultivating a broad-based, inclusive leadership team distributes the work and serves the ancillary, value added, benefits of fostering collaboration and nurturing leadership in others. Through a shared leadership approach many of the responsibilities being placed on the principal's back can be disseminated to others on the leadership team. As Fullan (2001) states, "Strong institutions have many leaders at all levels. Those in a position to be leaders of leaders . . . know they do not run the place. They know that they are cultivating leadership in others" (134). When schools realize the benefits of distributed leadership are reciprocal and see students as the primary recipients, the meaning of VAULT crystallizes.

Steve Farber (2004), a leading researcher and leadership trainer, supports the need for cultivating leadership in others stating, "Leadership is not a solo act; it doesn't happen in a vacuum. You're not going to change the world by yourself. It's your job to recruit, cultivate, and develop the Extreme Leaders in your midst" (176). It is by engaging in this vital win-win leadership approach that schools become empowered to achieve greatness!

The concept of sharing responsibly for the instructional program is not new. From schools with a coprincipalship to more extensive reframing of the principalship, distributive approaches have been presented as ways to improve instruction and also as a means to share ownership for advancing the school's academic mission. Eckman (2007) supports a divided principalship arrangement "as an organizational structure that addresses the increasing workload and time demands of the principal as well as the shortage of qualified applicants for the position" (313). Growing your own leadership team is just common sense for survival in a twenty-first-century principalship.

As the education community in the last decade has recognized the benefits of distributed leadership they have begun to tap the expertise of lead teachers, peer coaches, content specialists, and others campus leaders with specialized knowledge and skills to aid in the improvement of the school's instructional program. Support for the idea of distributed leadership has grown as school leaders at the local, state, and national levels look for ways to restructure the principalship.

Mayrowertz (2008) found in his study of distributed leadership that educational policy groups like the Council of Chief State Officers and the Education Commission of the States "have endorsed the idea of distributed leadership" (425). What has become clear is that effective instructional leadership is not the sole province of the principal but must tap the synergy available from within the organization for success. There may be a single individual perched at the top of the school's organizational chart but by "flattening" the school organization through a shared, distributed leadership model, the instructional vision can be more efficiently advanced.

Progress toward a more diversified approach to the management of the school's instructional goals is not a panacea for all schools. As Harris (2002) describes, "While it would appear from the research evidence that distributed leadership can be advantageous to school and teacher development, achieving it is far from easy" (7).

For starters, it is not easily defined. As University of Michigan researchers Camburn, Rowan, and Taylor (n.d.) discuss, there are two conceptual challenges attendant to distributive leadership: "(1) to identify the forms of leadership that are distributed among members of the school community, and (2) to identify members to whom these leadership functions can be distributed" (6). We simply have to purposefully and thoughtfully frame distributed leadership in an organizational context where it can flourish.

Accountability

So, you are asking, "What about accountability?" Let me be crystal clear; as we explore the time-related issues facing the principal and the reconfiguration of the instructional responsibilities on a campus, the instructional buck still stops on the principal's desk. She or he has to be directly answerable for the school's academic shortcomings or failures. The principal can, and should, broadly share the limelight of the school's successes with all stakeholders, but playing the blame game will never advance the school improvement agenda.

Within a distributed leadership approach there can be no mitigating the principal's accountability for what happens on his or her watch: no personal lack of awareness or "cluelessness" General Motors or Enron style for one's accountability for the school's success (Bolman and Deal 2003, 4). Simply put, the principal still has to be the leader and recognize and accept the fact that the accountability bull's eye is on his or her back for the success of the school's instructional program.

To be the instructional leader of a school requires that one engenders trust among the faculty and staff. Trust not only for maintaining democratic principles and doing the right thing for the right reason, but also for giving more than is expected of others. This does not mean one can use terms like *shared responsibility*, *collaboration*, and *distributed leadership* as euphemisms for shirking responsibility. The principal in a distributed leadership approach still has to be seen as "in charge" as well as one that "takes charge" of the instructional program. Additionally, the principal has to be actively involved in the day-to-day functions of the instructional program and intimately aware of the status of all steps being taken toward school improvement. Like the father who was asked by his daughter's boyfriend, "How did you raise such a wonderful girl?" The father answered, "I trust my daughter but I check the dickens out of her!"

Principals simply cannot abdicate their responsibility for the overall success of the school's instructional program in a misguided understanding of distributed leadership—they have to trust and verify the impact of their school's academic program on all students. The relative success of the school's academic program still rests with the person wearing the principal's nametag: the one who is unquestionably accountable.

Framework for Success:
The Keys to the Leadership Kingdom

Each of the keys will be presented in a similar format that allows for an examination of the issue as it relates to the overarching VAULT approach. Each chapter will begin with a Preflection scenario illustrative of the issue covered and designed to serve as a reflective anchor for the reader.

Once the stage has been set with the Preflection scenario, the remainder of the chapter will present the author's views and theory base related to the topic. Following the discussion of the chapter's key issue a reflection is included to encourage readers' synthesis of the key and its application to their practice. It is suggested that readers use the reflection as a tool for considering the key's potential for the recapture of their professional time and for tapping the leadership talents of others.

Keys for Unlocking the Vault (In You)

Outlined on the following pages are the keys that provide the framework for discussing the dual issues of time management and shared decision making. It is critical that the reader reflectively consider both the element of time and the distributed leadership aspect as the keys are fleshed out. The time factor without its being coupled to a change toward distributed leadership on your campus will only serve to frustrate you and your staff.

Also, it is important at the onset to mention that the issue of change will be a common thread throughout the discussion of distributed leadership. Self-directed change as well as cultivation of change within the leadership team are essential requisites for a successful transfer of power from an individual to a group.

Putnam (2000) emphasizes another important dimension to the importance of the organization—whether the organization is bonding (or exclusive) or bridging (or inclusive) (22). Bonding in organizations has the tendency to reinforce exclusive or homogenous groups, while organizations that display a bridging and inclusive nature embrace and include all individuals regardless of the perceived social divide. This book encourages school leaders to find ways to begin this "bridging" process and for becoming an inclusive Value Added Unified Leadership Team that embraces the leadership diversity of their campus's social capital.

And finally, readers must understand the existence of both internal and external power struggles that will challenge their restructuring of instructional leadership. Moving toward a transference of power from an individual to a leadership team takes visioning, goal setting, reflection, and at least initially, a pretty thick skin. Meaningful schoolwide change of this type requires a leadership team that is proactive in establishing the leadership parameters that can sustain their success.

The process presented in the following chapters is not a quick fix nor will it be successful without the support of other key stakeholders. What will be required are leaders who understand the change process, are able to clearly articulate the distributed leadership roles, and have perseverance and resilience in performing the principal's job.

An overview of the seven VAULT keys are presented to the reader as the following.

Key #1—Realizing that school leaders are time challenged and that conventional approaches to academic leadership produce unrealistic requirements for leaders. Throughout my career as a campus- and district-level administrator and while teaching in a university principal preparation program, I have encountered numerous excellent principals. When they can slow down enough to visit, I ask them what is the number one challenge they face in the principalship. Perhaps surprising to some, it is not high-stakes testing, No Child Left Behind, student discipline, campus security, paperwork, or providing a high-quality education to every student within limited budgets. Invariably principals respond that they simply do not have time to be the instructional leader they know they can, and should, be.

These are dedicated, well-trained professionals who carry the mantle of instructional leadership very seriously. They are putting in an incredible number of work hours each week, both at their school and with the unfinished work they take home.

These individuals are crying out for support and for new ideas that can be utilized to redirect their time and energy to the teaching and learning process. As chapter 2 unfolds it will provide backdrop for subsequent chapters by looking at the time issues facing all principals and construct a case for reassessing where time is currently spent and how the VAULT concept can begin to free up valuable minutes for the school's instructional team.

Key #2—Recognizing the reality of time management myths and how to overcome the time traps inherent in each. Numerous articles and books have been written on issues related to time management. Chapter 3 will provide support for the time management concepts that have value for the instructional leader. Additionally, this chapter will examine leadership fallacies like the glib response many principal job seekers use to endear themselves to interview committees: "I have an open-door policy" and "I am approachable for the staff 24/7." These are the unrealistic leadership promises that will be exposed as the principal seeks to find balance in his or her professional life.

The concept of monkeys on the leader's back as offered by Oncken and Wass (1974/1999) will forge the demarcation lines for exploring time and personal management. Oncken and Wass present three types of time issues: "boss-imposed time"; "system-imposed time"; and, "self-imposed time" as related to the interactions faced by leaders in an organization. With the first two—boss-imposed and system-imposed—the authors found little or no flexibility for the leader, leaving self-imposed time as the kind that can be considered for fine-tuning (3–4).

Working within the leadership's self-imposed time requires a resistance to the temptation to be all things to all people. Leadership teams failing to understand and control their limits will continually struggle in finding instructionally dedicated time.

Key #3—Admitting that micromanagement is a debilitating leadership addiction and a successful cure is creating a distributive leadership team that positively impacts the success of students. One of the worst maladies facing an instructional leader is his or her misguided need to touch every decision and to be involved in solving every problem. Instructional leaders smitten with an illness of this type of heroship are destined to a professional life that is frustrating and organizationally incapacitating.

Even the Lone Ranger understood that there was a need for a trusted companion like Tonto, and his marvelous horse Silver, when facing adversity and championing justice. School leaders, as a survival tactic, have to stop micromanaging and, instead, use the time for unifying and strengthening the school's leadership team by utilizing and trusting the knowledge and skills of others on the campus.

Key #4—Knowing that collaboration through distributive leadership can lead to improved academic performance through a Value Added Unified Leadership Team (VAULT) approach will lead to improved instructional support. Key #3 leads to Key #4. Once the leader held captive by the urge to "know all and be all" to everyone in the school begins to relinquish some positional power, then he or she can begin to forge a Value Added Unified Leadership Team. No where have I suggested this would be easy; I have only proposed that growing leadership in others—particularly instructional leadership—will serve to strengthen the span of organizational responsibilities while, at the same time, flattening the instructional aspect of the school and contributing to the creation of the community of learners.

Chapter 5 will provide the link between research on leadership teams and its meaning for the practitioner for strengthening the instructional program of their school. The value added aspect will be explored and strategic planning steps will be offered in a systematic process for (1) assessing the current state of instructional leadership (Where are we?); (2) identifying the gaps that exist between the current state and the desired state (Where do we want to go?); (3) considering alternatives and choosing among the possible actions (How do we get there?); and (4) assessing progress toward improved instructional leadership (How did we do?).

This planning cycle assumes that your campus and your leadership team will never "arrive" but are always planning for the improvement of the school's teaching and learning core. As my superintendent, Dr. Gerald Anderson, often wisely told me when I was a high school principal eager to improve every aspect of the school at once, "John, an inch is a cinch and a yard is too hard" (personal communication). The wisdom I captured from this seemingly simplistic comment was that school leaders have a vision for where they want to lead a campus but it still takes time. Freeing up that time is the essence of chapter 5 and of the book.

Key #5—Knowing how to facilitate the organization of a VAULT academic improvement collaborative will assist with the structuring of instructional improvement process tasks. Just as Key #3 leads into Key #4, the latter key leads into this one. Knowing that school leaders must change and knowing what they can consider changing to (VAULT leadership) are two important reveals. Knowing the "how" to change is quite another matter and will require readers to understand the systematic steps needed for successfully implementing a VAULT approach on their campus. Chapter 6 will provide principals with an organized and logical approach for understanding the VAULT process and the steps for successfully reorganizing the leadership work on their campus.

Key #6—Knowing that a motivated self leads to motivated others in the organization will invigorate the school with students becoming the academic beneficiaries. For principals to successfully incorporate the tenets of the VAULT approach requires a fundamental understanding of their own time management strengths and weaknesses. The VAULT strategies focus more on a leader building a team by cultivating the strengths of its members rather than trying to overcome deficient areas of his or her leadership skills.

Knowing oneself and understanding each team members' knowledge, skills, and dispositions are important for keeping the team energized and motivated for overall success. Successful leadership teams will model the instructional practices needed to provide a high-quality education for all students.

Key #7—Understanding that reflection is a key to continued renewal of the VAULT. Being able to step back and thoughtfully consider the progress being made by your VAULT is essential to continuous improvement. This requires that the team as well as individual team members review the organizational goals and gauge the improvements and deficits that have resulted from the team's efforts. Reflective practice gives the VAULT a deeper understanding of their campus's academic goal-attainment progress.

Reflective practice involves thoughtfully considering the team's attainment of the campus instructional goals and encouraging the deconstruction of events encountered in order to improve judgment and increase the predictable success of complex situations facing the school's leadership. This chapter 7 will encourage a reflective practice that looks at the team's practice through a scholar-practitioner theoretical lens as well as suggesting ways to become more reflective, in addition to looking at campus data, such as action research.

These keys, taken collectively, are designed to become an organizational catalyst for not only changing the way campuses are led, but also finding priceless minutes for the leader that can be utilized for instruction. Overcoming the organizationally imposed time demands such as central office and campus meetings, professional development opportunities, site-based and other stakeholder meetings, paperwork, budgeting, staffing, school support, and other student services–related requirements, will provide the time needed by busy principals to lead their school's distributed leadership team by forging a "value added" benefit to the instructional program.

CHAPTER TWO

~

Time Challenges Facing Twenty-First-Century School Leaders

Key #1—Realizing that school leaders are time challenged and that conventional approaches to academic leadership produce unrealistic requirements for the leader.

Preflection

Entering Principal Mike Middlin's office for the third time this week was the school's football coach, Ed Walker. Coach Walker not only had outstanding teams throughout his career, this year's team was no exception and was destined for the record books. At least partially responsible for the team's success was the ability of Coach Walker to assemble a high-quality coaching staff with a true commitment to their athlete's success in the classroom as well as the field of play. The principal's secretary could read frustration in the furled brow of the head coach and asked him if he was trying again to get a minute of Principal Middlin's time.

"Coach," as everyone fondly referred to him, was exasperated as the principal's secretary could tell. She had left at least five "While You Were Out" notes for the principal explaining that Coach needed a minute of the principal's time to discuss an urgent issue. As of this sweltering August afternoon, these reminders had fallen on deaf ears. Always chipper and helpful, Mrs. Jaster told Coach she would not let Mr. Middlin leave without his getting back to him.

Returning to the field house to prepare for the day's practice and an evening scrimmage with crosstown rival Springfield, Coach contemplated the dilemma he faced. Always a fierce competition, Springfield had a reputation for suiting up unsavory characters and for bringing an entourage of similarly nasty thugs comprising drop outs and gang bangers as their supporters. Coach Walker has always cherished clean sportsmanlike competition and held his squad to a high standard of personal conduct on and off the field.

Frankly, he was concerned for the safety of his players, coaches, and fans and desperately needed to confirm the games security plan with Principal Middlin. Just as an unthinkable visualization of what potentially could happen crossed his mind the phone rang. Answering the phone on the second ring Coach heard the lovable voice of the principal's secretary on the other end of the line. He thought, finally I can put this issue to the back burner and concentrate on the Xs and Os of tonight's scrimmage.

To his surprise, Mrs. Jaster reported that she was not able to "tie the principal down" and apologetically offered that Mr. Middlin had an important personal issue and had left campus. He had, she relayed, said he would put Coach first on his agenda the following morning and even bring donuts. When probed, she admitted the principal's son was having a birthday and Mr. Mullins had forgotten to get the cake and a present. Exasperated, Coach Walker sank back into his office chair to contemplate the potential for a disastrous scrimmage if a safety plan was not executed.

The next morning the two did meet but it was not to enjoy the donuts and play by play review of the previous night's scrimmage. Rather, the principal and coach were joined by the school superintendent and school board president for a conference call with the state's athletic council. It seems that, predictably, during the scrimmage some of the Springfield "fans" had taken umbrage to a late hit on their team's star running back late in the game. The situation on the field quickly escalated into a nightmare brawl scenario as the home team left the field. The aftermath left two coaches seriously injured. The chaotic situation required a significant law enforcement response once they were notified of the fight by a reporter covering the game for the local newspaper. Now the state's athletic league's executive board wanted to know why the game did not have sufficient security in place for a scrimmage that the host team should have anticipated would be a heated rivalry.

Introduction

Most school leaders I have visited with over the last couple of decades indicate they are strapped for time to spend in classrooms. To a person they realize their role is to be the instructional leader. They understand this role is the single most significant way they can impact student success and equity. There is for most of these highly capable leaders a real disconnect between what they were hired to do and the reality of the job.

The Role of Instructional Leadership

Readers will understand from the previous chapter that principals face considerable role ambiguity. A gap exists between the principal's job description and the actual day-to-day duties. Many authors have written on the importance of the position's instructional role. Lezotte, building on his seminal work with Dr. Ron Edmunds, Wilbury Brookhover, and others, has continued to define and refine the factors producing school success. Guiding school effectiveness in both the first and second generation of school success correlates is the role of principal as instructional leader. Lezotte and Pepperl (1999) state, "In an effective school, the principal acts as an instructional leader, effectively and efficiently communicating the mission to staff, parents, and students. The principal understands and applies characteristics of instructional effectiveness in the management of the instructional program" (107–108). As the principal's role as instructional leader became a central tenet for school effectiveness it became central to the preparation and professional development of school leaders.

The Interstate School Leaders Licensure Consortium's Standards for School Leaders reinforced this as crucial to the preparation of principals stating, "Effective school leaders are strong educators, anchoring their work on central issues of learning and teaching and school improvement" (ISLLC 1996, 5). Even the No Child Left Behind Act (2001) requires states to use Title II funds to be certain "principals have the instructional leadership skills to help teachers teach and students learn" (NCLB, 8).

As this framework for reforming the role of the principal matured, districts began to seek skilled instructional leaders for vacant principalships. This new era of instructional leadership has predictably placed significant demands for accountability for student success and equity on the principal as well as for the university programs that prepare them.

Many entities at the national, state, regional, and local levels are working to promote excellence in the preparation and ongoing mentoring of school leaders. From the federally funded Northwest Regional Educational Laboratory to groups like the Southern Regional Education Board, and foundations like the Wallace Foundation and the Bill and Melinda Gates Foundation, research continues to emphasize the principal as an instruction leader.

Redefined Role of Principal: VAULT(ing) Ahead

As it should be, the role of principal continues to be redefined as it should in a continuous improvement context. What the effective schools movement started with its emphasis of the principal being at the school's leadership pinnacle has matured to a more broad and inclusive definition of instructional leadership. Starratt (1995) discusses the transition of the principalship role as a movement away from "functional rationality" with its emphasis on managerial efficiency to viewing the principal's role as one of "substantive rationality" (9).

With substantive rationality school leaders focus on the school's desired end product by questioning the reasons, meaning, and value of the school's work. Schools led by a principal with a substantive rationality underpinning have shifted the leader's attention away from "heat, light, and ventilation" issues toward a focus on student academic success and equity.

Fulfilling the promise of transforming both principals' practice and school reform requires a community of learners who become a community of educational leaders. With the empowerment of others in the school family, the leader becomes a catalyst for effecting needed change. Ubben, Hughes, and Norris (2001) note this trend stating, "Even though the original models of instructional leadership were driven by the effective schools concept that placed the principal at the apex of learning, there is still relevance in considering the dimensions of that leadership as guides for establishing a shared leadership effort in which the principal serves as a *facilitator of the process* (35, emphasis in original). Principals who empower others through shared leadership move from the instructional position of "sage on the stage" to one of being an inclusive "guide on the side." The principal now has become what Cunningham and Cordeiro (2006) and others term the school's "lead learner" (206).

Value Added Unified Leadership

Background to the Value Added Approach
The role of principal has, without a doubt, become more complex. Working in twenty-first-century schools, the instructional leader is held more accountable than ever for student success. The principal's accomplishment of the school's delivery of a more rigorous and relevant curriculum is compounded by many other demanding roles and responsibilities.

These secondary functions often serve as a time "Catch-22" thwarting success in the principal's primary area of performance—teaching and learning. If the principal tends to instructional issues the wheels often come off in

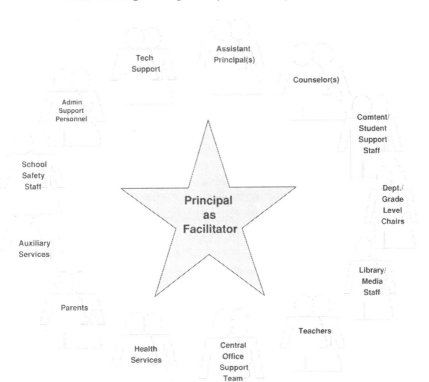

Figure 2.1. The Principal as Hub

another area of responsibility. Conversely, if the secondary "heat, light, and ventilation" issues are a priority, support for teaching and learning suffers.

This dilemma unfolds on a daily basis in schools across America. School leaders are under immense pressure to perform in a school venue that includes a multitude of job-related responsibilities that are often at odds with an instructional focus. Figure 2.1 illustrates the incredibly complex roles and expectations for a principal as evidenced in a sample of a principal's job description adapted from a posting for a high school principal in Illinois.

Sample Principal Job Description

Job Responsibility Overview
Responsible for the total program of the school, including activities that relate to teachers, pupils, educational programs, supplies, and equipment. The principal's primary responsibility is in the improvement of instruction.

A majority of the time is spent on curriculum and staff development through both formal and informal activities, establishing clear lines of communication regarding school goals, accomplishments, practices, and policies with parents and teachers. The duties and responsibilities of the principal include concerns for leadership/curriculum; supervision/evaluation/improvement; public relations; organization; accountability; information; and contract administration.

Supervision

Under broad supervision, this position supervises the associate principal, assistant principals, and all full-time and part-time building staff, including teachers, nurse, office and technical employees, counselors, speech therapist, lunchroom supervisors, substitute teachers, student teachers, program assistants, junior participants, hall monitors, police liaison, cooks, and custodians (implies a sharing of supervision).

Job Duties

- Gives leadership to development and improvement of the instructional programs.
- Organizes and develops a school climate that promotes adequate discipline of students, rapport with teachers, and understanding of parents to the end of an excellent learning environment.
- Cooperates with all appropriate administrative personnel, teaching staff, parents, students, and others in assuring the best education for all pupils, and coordinates efforts to this end.
- Accepts responsibility for providing the means for teachers to be successful through in-service training, counseling, and appropriate examples.
- Schedules time so that a minimum of 75 percent of the work year is devoted to instructional leadership.
- Screens candidates and makes employment recommendations to the assistant superintendent of human resources.
- Responsible for a positive public relations program with parents and community in general.
- Accepts the responsibility of acting as a liaison person in working with the parent teacher organization (PTO) and other stakeholder groups including parents, site-based and district-based committees, and others engaged in the school improvement process.
- Plans and organizes the use of school facilities in the best interests of the pupils and the community.

- Organizes the building in a functional sense so that a smooth operation in terms of programs, staff functioning, and pupil involvement is enhanced.
- Organizes and administers the school within the approved policies of the Board of Trustees.
- Ensures the safety of people involved with the school system and maintains the buildings, furnishings, books, and apparatus contained therein from damage and ensures proper care and cleanliness.
- Accepts the responsibility for accounting procedures in the areas of budget, all funds, and teacher attendance.
- Accepts responsibility for all reports and special duties assigned by or with the approval of the superintendent.
- Supervises attendance records and periodically reviews those records to ensure that school staff members are following federal and state requirements and reporting that data.
- Complies with all federal and state requirements regarding educational leadership and school improvement planning.
- Keeps the central office administration informed of all matters in the building that may have ramifications for the Board of Trustees or the district.
- Becomes knowledgeable of the provisions of all collective bargaining agreements to properly administer those provisions for which the principal is responsible.
- Performs all other duties commensurate with the position and that may be assigned.
- Directs and ensures supervision of all extracurricular activities.
- Evaluates the performance of all staff assigned under direct supervision.

The above description covers the most significant duties performed, but does not mention other duties that may be required.

Minimum Requirements
   Education: master's degree, appropriate licensure/certification
   Years of prior teaching: 5
   Years of administration: 5
   Contract period: 12 months, 260 days

Most of us get tired just reading the requirements for the principal's position in the sample above. It has truly evolved into a position requiring a high level of knowledge and specialized expertise, as well as a unique set of dispositions for handling the school's many publics. From instructional skills to knowledge of personnel management to budgeting to school safety, the principal has a rather large target placed on his or her back for accountability.

Overcoming the complexity of the principalship entails our looking at the position with a new set of assumptions. Among these is the most important assumption: one person cannot (and should not) be solely responsible for the success of the school's instructional program. Essential in this belief is the pivotal role that other key stakeholders should have in the design, implementation, and assessment of the school's academic program.

Although the instructional program should be the core function of the school, the reality for many schools is that it is relegated to a lesser-important status. This can be either purposeful, as in the case of states where football or basketball is "king" or as a result of autonomy for instructional decisions. Whatever the reason for marginalizing the instructional program, the principal still retains the accountability for results.

Broad-based School Leadership

The essence of moving from the constrained, independent principal to one who can be more fully actualized as the lead leader requires replacing dependence with a high level of trust for the principal's instructional decision making coupled with the district's support of site-based decision making. The ever-changing demands placed on public schools requires a concerted and systematic approach to the creation of learning communities that are nurtured through a shared commitment to commonly held beliefs and values focused on school improvement.

This commitment can only be accomplished with a principal's clear understanding of the importance of building a learning community. It is this unified "team" approach that distinguishes value added leadership from heroic leadership. Value added leadership provides the impetus for meaningful collaboration and contributions within the framework of an effective school.

Taking the principalship role into a realm of facilitator requires a new visioning of roles and responsibilities. In this perspective the principal accepts the ultimate accountability for the school's effectiveness as a facilitation professional. The principal becomes the hub for the school's VAULT leadership team as shown in figure 2.1. As the principal becomes the facilitator of the school's community of learning leaders he or she must accept this primary assumption: *one person cannot (and should not) be solely responsible for the success of the school's instructional program.* Reinventing the role of principal now casts the instructional leader as a catalyst, ultimately accountable for all of the job responsibilities, but willing to release power to other contributors within the leadership learning community.

Acceptance of the learning facilitator's responsibilities leads to a revisioned and restructured leadership team. The Value Added Unified Leadership Team is predicated on the additional assumptions that

1. The broad variety of the school's instructional capital must be recognized and valued;
2. in an effectual school, instructional leadership is widespread and focused on improving teaching-learning for *all* students.
3. When collegial leadership relationships are nurtured the community of learners engages in a continuous dialogue about pedagogy and praxis.
4. The existence of collegial leadership relationships serve to unify and strengthen the instructional program.

These assumptions support the principle that *one person cannot (and should not) be solely responsible for the success of the school's instructional program.* An examination of the assumptions that undergird this principle will begin to reveal the advantages of the VAULT approach to school leadership.

Assumption 1: The broad variety of the school's instructional capital must be recognized and valued. When a purposeful curricular reform initiative is undertaken, it must consider the context and needs of the organization making those transformations through the lens of democratic change. Combs (1988) suggests that one of the premises connected with successful and sustainable change is changing the belief system of those involved. Changing to a broader leadership community recognizes the need to alter the power structure in a school by valuing a more distributed approach. The result is a more resilient form of leadership guided by a shared vision for learning and systematic oversight of the curriculum. The school becomes a focused community of learners.

Zmuda, Kuklis, and Kline (2004) underscore the need for changing the belief system by challenging educators to "articulate and affirm the deeply held, defining beliefs that give purpose to their work" (39). Thus, these core beliefs serve as a school's nonnegotiable blueprint for guiding its work improving student success and equity. Where commonly held beliefs demonstrate a commitment to democratic practice, the contributions of all participants are valued.

Kincheloe (2005) clearly focuses the context of a democratic school to be one that considers "the moral, cognitive, affective, political, and social dimensions of what constitutes in the education of its students" (vi). Projecting the concepts of democratic practice into the school results in a community of learners who celebrate and nurture the expression of school improvement ideals contributed by internal and external stakeholders.

Within a school with shared democratic beliefs all participants are purposeful and committed to the instructional focus. Kincheloe (1999) finds that democratic purpose affects the teaching-learning process in three interrelated ways: "(1) teaching in a democratic workplace—teacher self-direction/empowerment; (2) the creation of democratic classrooms—developing student input into the nature of their own education; and (3) teaching for democratic citizenship—building a democratic society" (73). Inherent in this view is a belief that the efficacy of democratic principles originates within the discourse required to provide all students with improved educational opportunity.

Assumption 2: In an effectual school, instructional leadership is widespread and focused on improving teaching-learning for all students. Leadership from a distributed perspective enhances the democratic practice by supporting teachers in the delivery of a relevant and rigorous curriculum. Henderson (1999) maintains that the practice of democratic curriculum leadership will result in "a very specific and challenging transformative agenda" for schools (12).

Although curriculum improvement approaches abound in education, they are often prescriptive and tend to discount the uniqueness of schools, classrooms, and students. When the specific context and unique needs of the learners are aligned through specialized curriculums and instructional approaches, educational quality will improve.

This progress can best be lead by a leadership team whose support for democratic practice permeates the school. But school leaders must be cognizant that making substantive change will take their time and unrelenting focus. A move toward distributed leadership is more than just claiming the designation; the change is more complex than it appears, as we will see in subsequent chapters. It is much more than just the broadening of the leadership team or changes in the organizational structure. It is truly a new way of looking at the school world through a distributive leadership paradigm.

Assumption 3: When collegial leadership relationships are nurtured the community of learners engages in a continuous dialogue about pedagogy and praxis. As this pioneering VAULT approach is implemented, school leaders must adequately train those involved in the transformation and resist the pressures to revert to a "same leaders leading the same way" default. Or, a comment I have heard in many organizations when leaders changed and new initiatives were tried, "This too shall pass." These negative forces can best be overcome with reflection and communication.

To ensure a smooth transition to distributed leadership the VAULT must be able to create an environment free from turf wars and sacred cows. This requires patience and the leadership team's ability to listen, learn, and lead. Leaders must build open lines of communication based on an open exchange of ideas. By modeling active listening the VAULT demonstrates the value of dialogue, which is a hallmark of reflective practice and leadership. The result, over time, is the development of a community of learners who feel safe ownership for improving their practice.

Assumption 4: The existence of collegial leadership relationships serve to unify and strengthen the instructional program. The vision, mission, and goals of a school are often mitigated by an organizational structure that is at best dispassionate and at worst oppositional to the innovative change. Recognizing this political struggle, Wong (2001) posits, "In contrast to transformative vision, once new ideas are mediated through institutional processes they become integrated into existing frameworks and are disarmed of their transformative punch" (6). Wong continued by noting the struggle a leader faces in bridging the gap between transformative ideas and politics is not "an insurmountable barrier" (136).

Introducing meaningful change requires the VAULT to deftly acknowledge the past and, at the same time, maintain a clear focus on the research-based, democratic ideals necessary for effective instructional practice. Once the distributive leadership genie is out of the proverbial bottle the VAULT must be committed to the fulfillment of the school's instructional vision. This requires reflective dialogue by all stakeholders.

Reflective questions make it possible for a VAULT to reflect on the school's current state and its preferred future. Through these crucial conversations schools as learning communities continually assess where they are, where they need to be in the future, how they get there, and how they will know when they have met their goals. To engage the leadership team in this dialogue, ask questions like the following:

- What is the most important instructional goal for us to focus on this week (month, semester, etc.)?
- How does this align with our school's instructional vision and mission?
- Where do we need to position ourselves instructionally to accomplish this and other goals?
- How will we use triangulated data evidence to determine where we are next week (month, semester, benchmark date, end of year/ course)?
- How can the VAULT be better tomorrow than we were today?

Conclusion

Chapter 2 has provided the historical backdrop for subsequent chapters by looking at the time issues facing principals and constructing the case for the need for reassessing where time is currently spent and how the VAULT concept can begin to free up valuable minutes for the instructional team. Factors important to this transformation are democratic practice centered on instructional goals and ongoing dialogue focused on the improvement of teaching and learning. Reflective practice then becomes a hallmark for the VAULT and larger learning community.

Chapter Reflection

Through the lens of a practitioner, revisit the situation faced by both the principal and coach in the chapter's Preflection. Consider the underlying issues that were symptoms of larger organizational issues by reflecting on the trigger questions that follow.

1. Did the principal's control of the campus decision-making processes limit his ability to focus on instructional issues?
2. Did the principal's focus on secondary issues—ones that might be on the job description but outside the instructional focus—cause a Catch-22 and contradict the principal's primary area of performance—teaching and learning?
3. How would the situation that evolved been different if (1) the leadership capacity of the school had included the coach and empowered him to resolve the potential safety concerns without the blessing of the principal? or (2) the principal had a laser focus on the attainment of the school's instructional mission?

CHAPTER THREE

~

Principal Time Management

Key #2—Recognizing the reality of time management myths and how to overcome the time traps inherent in each.

Preflection

Principal Suzuki sat in her office contemplating the day's events. How could the buses already have run when it seems like I just got out of my car and entered the building to start the day, she mused. Indeed the day had flown by with the typical and endless blur of events she had reconciled herself to expect. Starting with the fight on the morning bus the day had gone from bad to worse with a litany of student, teacher, and parent interruptions. But this was commonplace and days such as this were what Pat Suzuki had come to expect during her five years in the principalship.

Mentally beaten down, Pat's train of thought drifted toward her goal of going back to the university and working on her doctorate. Always a goal, she thought working on a terminal degree would at least give her an audience with whom to commiserate—surely all principals faced the same unrealistic expectations on their time: too much to do and never enough hours in the day to do all the tasks. She had been telling herself she would begin the doctoral program for the last seven years—when she had the time.

As she pondered her dilemma someone knocked on her door. Opening the door tentatively—she never knew who or what to expect—she saw the superintendent. Dr. Sandra Swanson had been superintendent of schools for the Sturford schools for many years. Always looking for the best and the brightest, she had chosen and mentored Pat Suzuki because she recognized her talent and her knowledge of middle school curriculum and instruction.

Entering the office, Dr. Swanson was taken aback by the demeanor of her middle school principal. Having never seen Pat so dejected, she asked what was troubling her and offered to be an active listener. Responding in a flood of bent-up frustrations, Pat Suzuki, determined not to get emotional, responded with a recap of the day's events from the fight to the parent advocate in the admission, review, and dismissal (ARD) meeting threatening to contact the Justice Department, to the infighting within the social studies department—she was just having a bad day.

The wisdom reflected in Dr. Swanson's response was one of a seasoned leader who knew how to begin the de-escalation of the problem with a collaborative, empathic ear. "I know you have thought about these issues—you probably lay awake at night trying to find solutions. Talk to me about your thoughts."

Relieved to have an understanding supervisor, Pat Suzuki confided that she just felt like she was not just burning out but emotionally burning up. Her life was consumed with school-this and school-that and she never found over two connected minutes for reflection nor was she actualized as the instructional leader. "I just feel like I need a renewal pill," she said.

Superintendent Swanson listened thoughtfully and resolved not to offer her own solutions for getting some of the "monkeys" off Pat Suzuki's back. When she did respond she said, "You know, Pat, you remind me so much of myself. There never seemed to be enough hours in the day, days in the week—you know what I'm saying. One day I got some very good advice from a trusted colleague about focusing on what's important. I know what is important to you here at school but what is it that, to use your term, provides that 'renewal pill' in your career?"

Pat did not hesitate and responded that she had always admired Dr. Swanson's ability to achieve so many career and personal goals. Dr. Swanson was at the pinnacle of the district as superintendent, had raised three great kids, had a doting husband and great marriage, and was active in the community. Her goal, she admitted to Dr. Swanson, was to someday realize a lifelong goal of having a doctoral degree. She had been a first-generation college graduate and knew the power of an education.

Dr. Swanson simply responded, "Well, why haven't you started a doctoral program? Every year you put it off means it will still be three years away. At some point you have to put action steps to the goals you hold for yourself, in your personal and professional life." Pat Suzuki sat stunned at the seemingly obvious advice she had just been given. She assured Dr. Swanson she would immediately begin the process of putting things into a prioritized perspective.

Introduction

Numerous articles and books have been written on issues related to time management. This chapter will provide support for the time management concepts that have value for the instructional leader. By examining nonproductive uses of time that have limited impact on a campus, these myths will be exposed for what they are: time adversaries.

What exactly is a *time adversary*? Time adversaries are like the glib response that many principal job seekers use to endear themselves to an interview committee. Wanting to appear to be a participatory leader with an open communication style they claim, "I have an open-door policy." That response might get you the job but an open-door policy will also, assuredly, be a nonproductive use of your time unless it is harnessed. And that is what a time adversary does to the instructional focus of a school leader: it redirects the principal's time and energy away from the important work of the school—the teaching and learning process.

In the pages that follow we will look at some of the time adversaries alive and well in many schools. By exposing these myths for what they are—time adversaries—we can begin to look at ways to redirect the minutes saved toward instructional issues.

Time Adversary #1:
I'll Have More Time Tomorrow

Oddly enough, I have found many individuals, including school leaders, who have somehow rationalized that tasks and responsibilities can be put off until mañana—an indefinite horizon of time. The older one gets the more one realizes the fallacy of believing that things can be put off until tomorrow or "someday."

We have to accept the reality that each of us, for the time we walk this earth, have the same measure of time. Sixty seconds in a minute, sixty minutes in an hour, twenty-four hours in a day, fifty-two weeks in a year—all of us are equal in this sense.

This time reality is heightened by the fact that our lives our getting more complex. We know we are experiencing dramatic changes in the demands being placed on principals and school leaders as we discussed in chapter 1.

When we layer on top of our professional life stressors the equally hectic personal lives we live, we are burning the proverbial candle at both ends.

Many school leaders are, obviously, raising families and serving their communities in a variety of ways. Some are returning to universities to pursue a terminal degree or advanced certifications or licenses. In the last few decades many educators are now realizing they are becoming primary caretakers for elderly parents and relatives. These and other situations all serve to lay claim to the minutes in your day. Putting things off until mañana is a luxury we cannot afford.

School leaders have to come to grips with the reality that something has to change. To begin this journey the school leader must accept the fact there is no magical dust that can be sprinkled over our daily lives and, mysteriously, what we wish to accomplish will be completed. It is this gap between "want to" and "will be" that we can work on.

Organizing, Prioritizing, and Delegating

To overcome the temptation to defer until mañana to commence a project, consider a process for prioritizing as the first step. To help you and your distributed leadership team sort through the innumerable issues that impact your collective time, consider using a decision-making chart like the one shown in figure 3.1 as a process for handling tasks on your campus. Some of the work can be handled immediately, some should be delegated to other VAULT members, and some can be deferred while you gather additional information. Each task is efficiently either quickly handled, delegated, or deferred. Let's look at each of these process steps as pictured in figure 3.1. Utilizing a process like the one in figure 3.1 can assist the VAULT in distributing the workload and staying focused on the team's core responsibility for the improvement of teaching and learning on the campus.

As the leader on the campus it is indispensable that you learn to turn loose of ownership for every decision. When a new task is presented, a critical initial decision point requires the leader to either take no action, handle the issue, or delegate it to a member of the VAULT or other individual. Those items you have chosen to delegate must be monitored with a "trust but verify" approach. In other words, trust the subordinate to handle but have a reporting system in place to monitor his or her progress toward the completion of the task.

Another useful tool for the VAULT to consider is one that identifies primary and secondary levels of responsibility for major tasks. Important initiatives can be processed using a chart like the one in table 3.1 that estab-

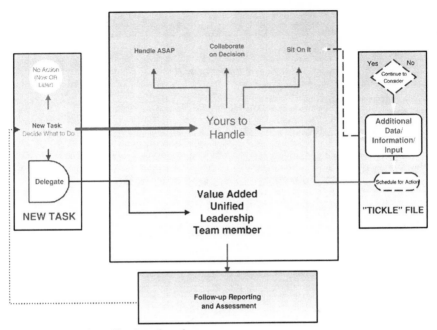

Figure 3.1.   Task Facilitation Flowchart

lishes primary, secondary, and assistance responsibilities. By utilizing a task responsibility chart, the principal can, in a very streamlined manner, utilize the members of the VAULT to accomplish a major task. Additionally, the empowered team members with a primary responsibility know there are others they can look to for support and assistance. This frees the principal from having to be the go-to person for every decision.

A Word about Procrastination

The connotation held by most of us for the word *procrastination* is one of a person who is not decisive. We need a decision but cannot get the person to, as the idiom says, "fish or cut bait." In reality, I think we all have the procrastination gene. We can find every available excuse for putting decisions off for "just a few more days" or until we have "more time" to decide.

Usually the decisions school leaders put off are the ones that they anticipate will be problematical, as with returning that phone call to the newspaper reporter doing a story on some salacious school-related issue. These feelings are all clues that the temptation to procrastinate is creeping into our psyche. Burka (1983) describes two ways procrastination can cause us

Table 3.1. Task Responsibility Matrix

Utopia High School

TASK:
Commencement

	Dean	Lewis	Baker	Mason	Chpra	Wilson	Chance
Speaker	A	P	S	A	A	A	A
Invocation	S	P	A	A	A	A	A
Valedictory Address	A	S	P	A	A	A	A
Salutatory Address	A	P	S	A	A	A	A
Programs	A	A	P	A	A	A	S
Facility	A	P	A	A	A	S	A
Security	A	S	P	A	A	S	A
Audiovisual	A	A	A	P	A	A	S
Parking	A	S	P	A	A	A	A
Stage Guests	A	P	A	A	A	A	S
Practice	A	S	P	A	A	A	A
Orchestra/Band/Choir	A	S	P	A	A	A	A
Emergency Services	P	S	A	S	A	A	A
Diploma Distribution	S	A	A	P	A	A	A

P = Primary Responsibility
S = Secondary Responsibility
A = Assistance

problems: "First, delaying may lead to external consequences ranging from innocuous (a library fine for late books) to severe (losing a job or jeopardizing a marriage). Second, people who procrastinate may suffer internal consequences, feelings that range from mild irritation to intense condemnation and despair" (5).

All of us fall somewhere along this continuum of internal and external feelings and possible consequences for procrastination. If each of us has genetic material for procrastinating alive in our being, how do we overcome the temptation?

One approach for conquering our tendency to drag our feet when approaching some tasks is to use the "pizza" technique. Visualize a large pizza (I have pepperoni in my mind but you choose the topping of your choice). If one attempts to eat the pizza without cutting it first into slices it becomes unmanageable and very messy. But if the pizza is cut into six or eight separate pieces we have a pie we can methodically overcome.

Taking the pizza analogy to our practice, we can understand that small steps can lead to our accomplishing large tasks more easily. The undertakings you are avoiding can best be accomplished by breaking the project into smaller tasks. You will find, as most of us in procrastination recovery programs understand, that the first step is the most difficult. But we also know we must take actions if we are to accomplish our vision.

We can take the pizza technique and apply it to the earlier example of a reluctance to return a call to the newspaper reporter. You remember, the one wanting to do a story about a salacious school-related issue. As the school leader you understand reporters are just doing their job. They have deadlines just like you do and bosses demanding results just as you do. You realize you cannot avoid the inevitable and you understand the wisdom for not getting on the media's wrong side, so you begin to take action.

Systematically, you start by setting a time to return the call. Next you look up the phone number and place it by your phone. Then you think about what you are likely to be asked and determine what you can and cannot tell the reporter. When the time comes you make the call.

You have just broken the task into at least four steps. You have more easily avoided the pitfalls associated with procrastination. Additionally, you avoided the external and internal consequences pointed out previously.

Time Adversary #2:
Your Shoulders Aren't Broad Enough

Most principals want to be available to their constituents: parents, teachers, students, and other stakeholders. This is a good thing. But the devil may be in the details of how one interacts with various publics. Too often an eager principal will unwittingly fall victim to a time adversary malady caused by monkeys leaping onto his or her back from multiple directions.

These "monkeys" are the problems, concerns, and issues that people inside and outside the school lay at the feet of a principal. These well-intending individuals have the expectation that the leader can solve all their problems. Like Dorothy and the Tin Man, Lion, and Scarecrow in the *Wizard of Oz*, everyone lays troubles at the feet of the leader.

The leader, wishing to be accommodating and demonstrate a supernatural ability to solve all the problems, makes the mistake of accepting these problems as his or her own to solve. The amalgamation of nondelegated monkeys being transferred to the principal's back—from the now lighter backs of others—is an impossible load for anyone to shoulder.

This time adversary can be untangled if the principal understands that Stephen Covey (1994) has it right when he says, "The main thing is keeping the main thing the main thing" (75). By coupling this sage advice with strategies for keeping the monkeys at bay and on others' backs the school leader will emerge with both more available time and a more empowered community of learners.

The concept of monkeys on the leader's back was originally penned by Oncken and Wass in 1974 for the *Harvard Business Review*. Considered a classic and one of the most popular articles published by this journal, it was reprinted in 1999 with commentary by Stephen Covey. Oncken and Wass found that others in the organization often place their burdens on the leader's back (3). Ultimately, if the leader decides to solve all of the problems, we have our first major time adversary to address: your shoulders are not that broad.

If you are the instructional leader then *be* the leader by empowering others to solve their own problems. The principal must resist the temptation to be all things to all people. Remember the quotation, "Give a man a fish; you have fed him for today. Teach a man to fish; and you have fed him for a lifetime"? This statement translated to building a Value Added Unified Leadership Team means you should nurture leadership in others by modeling problem ownership.

Problem solving one's own challenges builds individuals who can become value added assets to your school. Conversely, if you just solved their problems for them they will always be dependent of you and never release the leader within themselves. Concisely, to avoid this time adversary avoid accepting any monkeys—tamed or not—and instead, give others an opportunity to join the VAULT leadership team.

This does not mean you are not there to listen and guide others toward effective decision making. But it does mean a leader has to resist being lured into owning other peoples' problems. Leadership teams failing to understand and control the monkeys placed on them will limit their effectiveness and success with job number one, the success of all students.

Time Adversary #3:
People Keep Interrupting My Day

For most principals this is a bodacious problem. From the time you lock your car in the parking lot to the time you turn out the office lights at the end of the day, people tax your instruction time in all sorts of ways. Coworkers, superiors, subordinates, family members are just a few of the interrupters principals face each day. You cannot escape them but you can tame the fiend.

To start claiming less-interrupted time, Dr. Dru Scott (1980) suggests tracking your demands and interruptions. Follow this advice for one week during the semester. It can be done on a simple chart or in your day planner, or electronically on the district's meeting scheduler. Be sure to include the type of interruption, its duration, and level of importance (for example, Urgent, Important, Not Important) related to your instructional focus. Find a tracking system that works for you; it can be very revealing when you are searching for answers to the question of where the time went.

Once you have a sampling of interruption data reflect on how these interruptions are impacting your day. Start by considering whether the previous week was, indeed, pretty typical. Then begin analyzing who it is that seems to be tapping your time the most in this manner. Are the reasons valid or could they have been handled in a different way such as delegation? How important were these reasons? Were they individuals sticking their heads in your office to say "hello" or to "ask you a quick question"? Ask yourself whether the interruptions were important related to the time available to dedicate toward improved instruction.

Dealing with the Interrupter
I doubt whether the people who interrupt the work of the principal are being thoughtless but they might be unaware. In any case, the interrupter is making demands on your time and steps must be taken to interdict the practice.

In any organization there is a superordinate–subordinate pecking order and how you approach responding to the interrupter will look different depending on the individual's placement on the organizational chart. There are also a number of others who can be counted on to be the next interrupter, such as parents and community members.

We will discuss these in two groups. The first grouping are those more easily dealt with: your internal subordinates and colleagues, and the external public. We'll call this group the "minor interrupters." The second demarcation of interrupters are those you see as your bosses: those who you report to or have a high status on the organizational chart. We'll label this group the "major interrupters." The minor and major nomenclature is just a means of demarcation between those elevated in the organization and those on a similar or lesser rank on the organizational ladder.

Minor Interrupters
The minor interrupters are, by far, the most menacing group clamoring for your instructional minutes. They come in a vast array of guises from the colleague who wants to commiserate with you to the custodian who did not get the delivery of new mop heads this week. They wreak havoc on the instructional

time of the principal and the VAULT. They are the ones who lie in wait to ambush you as soon as you emerge from your office.

The good news is that these are, relatively speaking, the easiest ones to deal with in your school. As simple as it sounds, one must use a very directive approach when dealing with these time adversaries. They will plunder your valuable instructional minutes if you do not deal with them firmly.

The direct approach starts and ends with your instructional focus. How you are seen in "walking the walk" will speak volumes to those who make demands on your time. Learn to deal with these time detractors with tact and unswerving commitment to instructional time. Here's how.

Start by communicating to anyone within the reach of your words that instruction is the most important topic on the school's agenda. As the leader you will enforce this imperative by your actions and words. It may take time but people inside and outside the organization will begin to receive the message.

As one colleague I worked with put it, you have to "tell it like it is not how it ain't!" Heeding his advice takes both diplomacy and candor. Suppose a teacher on your campus catches you as you are heading to a classroom to do an instructional walk-through. She states, "I had a really rough time refinancing my mortgage to lower my interest rate." How do you respond?

My advice is to be direct and polite. Respond by telling the teacher, "Your dilemma sounds complicated but not as complex as the physics lesson I am on my way to observe. Let's talk after work about your situation." Responding in this manner not only shows a concern for the individual and their circumstance, it also reinforces your focus on instruction.

Major Interrupters

We all have had situations when the boss was the one coming unannounced into our inner sanctum. This situation calls for a vastly different approach from one with a colleague with a similar position or a subordinate. It is obvious that you should normally not tell the boss, "I am busy, please schedule an appointment with my administrative assistant." What you can do is listen to what the boss has come to say. Respond with a statement like, "I am glad to hear the district's financial audit is going well. I imagine your making me aware of this is more important than the department meeting I am late for."

You are thinking, I could never say something like that to my superintendent! Certainly not without it negatively impacting my annual appraisal. My response would be that of course you can. You were hired to lead a campus and be the instructional leader. Your standing up for what you believe in will always, in the final analysis, be seen as a strength. You have just sent a conscious message that will be received as a strong point and, at the same time, make the individual more aware of your instructional-related focus and time. I never said dealing with interrupters would be easy.

As you reflect, be sure to distinguish between what is "important" and what you view as "urgent." Understand that urgent is not necessarily important. Important issues are ones that keep you and your VAULT's eyes on school improvement.

Whether we are talking about major or minor interrupters the message remains the same. On our campus we have an instructional focus and, as principal, I will protect the time we have to support our learning community.

Time Adversary #4:
The "Paperwork Thing" Is Getting in My Way

For every administrator there is a significant amount of paperwork that rests on our desk or resides on our computer crying for attention. Our society has taken paperwork to a new level and it is increasingly in conflict with instructional time. If we consider that Lincoln's powerful Gettysburg Address was only 261 words in three paragraphs while President Obama's 2009 perhaps equally powerful inaugural speech was 2,406 words, we have to wonder if we aren't creating our own monster of paperwork.

How can we tame this ever-increasing amount of paperwork so we have time to dedicate to instructional issues? How can we deal with the cascade of paperwork coming into our office? Let's look at some typical paperwork problems: mail and memos, reports, and filing.

Mail and Memos

Incoming
True story: as a young administrator I asked one of the veteran principals how he managed to handle what seemed at the time to be an incredible amount of paperwork. I witnessed a blitz of letters, "While You Were Out" messages, and a countless number of other artifacts coming into this principal's office. Yet, his desk always seemed to be tidy and he never seemed as harried as one would expect. He looked me in the eye and said, "John, I know what I have to act on, the other pieces of mail are stacked on the side of my desk. If I have not received a follow-up from the sender in three weeks, it goes in the trash. I figure if it was important they will have contacted me about the status." While I am not inclined to encourage the reader to follow this paperwork practice, I admit there were times I did surreptitiously apply the principle.

Let's consider more viable approaches to handling mail, memos, and the like. Your first line of defense against the barrage of paper and electronic messages crossing your desk is your administrative assistant. Schools are staffed with the most dedicated and industrious secretarial talent in the world. Maximize the use of administrative assistants by valuing their knowledge and skills and by trusting their judgment and confidentiality.

Your administrative assistant should have access to all the mail that is routed to you, even information that is considered confidential. This person can greatly reduce your having to "touch" mail or e-mails that are either of no consequence (junk) or requests that can be handled more efficiently by others in the organization. Only the important things should reach your desk for your action using the decision chart in figure 3.1.

But, you say, I have personal e-mails coming in that I don't want my administrative assistant to read. My response, your district's e-mail service is no place for you to use for personal business. One, if you engaged in personal correspondence at school you are creating your own time adversary and detracting from valuable instructional minutes. Two, from a legal perspective, all of your e-mails whether school-related or personal may be releasable through an open records request.

Outgoing

Outgoing mail and memos are also a consumer of your instructional time. Once, using our decision-making process, it is yours to handle, respond by handling it ASAP, collaborating on the response and method, or "sitting on it."

Once you have done the initial screening of the correspondence and made a decision to respond, think about using tips provided by Alec Mackenzie (1997). Among Mackenzie's recommendations are the following. Consider other ways to respond to the written correspondence such as making a telephone call. In our era this might include the options of e-mailing, texting, sending a "tweet," or other forms of instant messaging. Another tip of his is to make your correspondence concise and to the point. As was noted with the reference to Lincoln's Gettysburg Address, we can deliver significant meaning in a short response.

Mackenzie's final tip would be to keep a file of sample letters for recurring situations. There are many sets of school-related examples available that can be modified and personalized for your use. An example of this would be keeping a letter of recommendation frame so it can be quickly individualized for the numerous requests school leaders get to support their graduates for scholarships and such (Mackenzie 1997, 161).

Reports

We all are asked to prepare, read, and/or analyze reports related to our work. Many excellent publications are available on a multitude of school-related topics. Whether received in the mail, accessed on the Internet, or as part of your ongoing professional development, they can be the source of a wealth of school improvement information.

As the reader of these publications, always start by examining the abstract or executive summary section. Lengthy reports almost always start with this type of overview and provide a synopsis of the contents. From your review of this section of the report you can quickly determine the merits of its contents. Again, use the decision chart to take an action (note: no action is action). By doing this you are rewarded by reading only articles or reports that have merit and saving instructional minutes by not reading those with little value.

Filing

For most of us, a filing system—whether paper or electronic—is a matter of personal choice. Not a choice of whether to keep good files but "how" we manage the huge volume of pieces of paper and electronic information. It stands to reason if we use our decision-making schema from figure 3.1 that the easiest filing is in the proverbial circular file. If it is not actionable, either now or later, then eliminate the clutter by disposing of it.

The most important thing to remember about any filing system is that you should be able to access the file you need—either paper or electronic—in less than two minutes. Impossible you say. I disagree and, with a little advanced planning, I think you can also learn to be a file master.

Work with your administrative assistant to find a complementary system for filing items systematically. One that is understandable and useable for all members of the VAULT. Kerry Gleeson (1998) provides a methodology for managing three types of paper or electronic files: (1) working files, (2) reference files, and (3) archive files.

Working Files

Gleeson describes these files as those containing six classes of files. The first, "fingertip information," files are those with readily available information like emergency phone tree charts, security alarm codes, and frequently used items like local and state educational organizations' contact information.

The second classification are held in a file captioned "items to be discussed." These are the items you have chosen to handle by opting to collaborate on the decision (see table 3.1). Place the items in this file category that will be agenda items for meetings with the VAULT or other collaborators you will consult.

The third of Gleeson's groupings is titled, "routine functions." As the file nomenclature suggests, place items of a routine nature in these files. Recurring tasks from ideas for the principal's weekly bulletin to a separate folder for the next parent teacher organization meeting should be filed here.

The fourth classification of files is one Gleeson titles, "current projects." Each current project should be a file that can be easily accessed. An example would be a file for managing ongoing curriculum revisions on your campus. It might also be one for the restroom remodeling project and containing architectural renderings or Americans with Disabilities Act (ADA) reference materials.

The fifth file type is one that is extremely important, the "tickle file." This file type, according to Gleeson, is set up in two sections. The tickle file is segmented by month and also within each month are 31 files, for each day. As a school leader, you will find this file type to be indispensable. Working with your administrative assistant you can devise a system to preview what is forthcoming that needs to be handled by a certain date. You will always be aware of important meetings or due dates and be able to stay abreast of all your more predictable tasks.

The last filing system is the trusty old alphabetical file. Gleeson recommends using these files for the more nonroutine items. Filing of these items alphabetically will still take some communication with your administrative assistant. Deciding whether "financial audit" goes under F or A will require some communication (Gleeson, 45–46).

In choosing to file the item as any of the six Gleeson file types, strive to only handle it once. Remember, your files whether paper or electronic should be readily accessible within two minutes or less. If your working files are established in a systematic manner you will overcome one time adversary.

Reference Files

School administrators amass a large volume of files needed for reference. These files range from professional development presentations to legal issue updates. The ability to access these files within our two minute standard dictates that they are ordered and subordered in some fashion.

Taking the legal reference file as an example, there should be one section, from a partial filing cabinet drawer to several drawers, that contains files related to legal issues. Within the legal heading will likely be subfiles on a variety of legal issues for ready reference. It is recommended that the subfiles be arranged in an alpha order. As an example, the first subfolder may be files on the Americans with Disabilities Act on to the end of the legal section with, perhaps, a Workers' Compensation folder.

Archive Files
Gleeson offers advice for the creation of archival files. These are two sets of files: one for your personal use, the other to be available for use by others. Essentially these sets of files achieve the same functionality: accessibility at a later date (Gleeson, 43–51).

An example of archive files that would be personal in nature would be job-related actions you have taken, such as a Title IX investigation. It might be many years after the investigation that your files could be subpoenaed. It should, once again, only take a couple of minutes for you to retrieve needed information.

Archival files that are of a more public nature would be files needed to be accessed by staff for a variety of reasons. They could be student-related cumulative files needed by staff to make decisions about students. These files could be more mundane in nature, such as model lesson plan examples for teachers to use.

As a footnote: all files can become voluminous over time. Systematically purge your files each year. Retain current information and remove outdated files to an external storage site or discard obsolete files. Caution: pay close attention to your district's records retention policy prior to destroying any of your documents.

Conclusion

All school leaders face incomprehensible demands on their time. The complexity of the work for the instruction leader requires a systematic response for meeting their job-related requirements. This chapter has discussed some of the biggest time adversaries that deflect valuable minutes away from the VAULT's instructional emphasis. Other barriers will be covered in subsequent chapters with a sole purpose of allowing school leaders to get into classrooms and provide direction for the school's curriculum and instruction.

Chapter Reflection

Pat Suzuki, our principal in the Preflection, assured her superintendent she would immediately begin the process of putting her personal and professional life into perspective. From the suggestions offered in this chapter, what suggestions would you give to Pat and other busy school leaders to reclaim instructional minutes related to the following:

1. Resisting the urge to accept the "monkeys" others are trying to place on your back.
2. Controlling the number of interruptions that negatively impact instructional practice.
3. Establishing systems for managing the "paperwork thing" that ties school leaders to their desk.
4. Deciding how to prioritize tasks with a sound decision-making process.
5. Overcoming the temptation to procrastinate and get difficult tasks off the to-do list.

CHAPTER FOUR

~

Avoiding the Pitfalls of Micromanagement

Key #3—Admitting that micromanagement is a debilitating leadership addiction and a successful cure is creating a distributive leadership team that positively impacts the success of students.

Preflection

Pat "Skip" Paulson, superintendent of the Springvale School District, arrived at work just before 8:00 a.m. as was his routine. Checking with Marge Delaney, his administrative assistant, as he approached his office, he was given the usual assortment of "While You Were Out" messages. Marge Delaney had worked for Dr. Paulson for over thirty years and they had developed a tremendous confidence and respect for each other. Trust had always been the bedrock of their relationship.

As she always could be counted on to do, Marge had deftly handled many of the calls and e-mails and efficiently prioritized the remainder for Dr. Paulson's actions. Pointing to one of these items, Marge mentioned that the call from the education reporter for the *Daily Progress* seemed to be rather urgent. Something, she said, related to an ADA complaint from one of the district's elementary librarians that had "leaked" to the newspaper.

Predictably, Dr. Paulson asked Mrs. Delaney if she had routed the issue to the assistant superintendent for human recourses. Also quite predictable, Marge responded that she had sent Tim Morgan a copy of the request. She had already tentatively scheduled a brief meeting with Mr. Morgan and

41

Superintendent Paulson for 8:30 a.m. Agreeing to the meeting, Skip Paulson began to review the other matters Marge had handed to him as he entered his office to begin his day.

Promptly at 8:30 Tim Morgan was ushered into the superintendent's conference room to discuss the newspaper reporter's request for an interview. Dr. Paulson began by asking Tim for a briefing on the substance of the ADA complaint. It seems the librarian filing the complaint had chronic fatigue syndrome and had requested to be able to take two one-hour naps during the day as prescribed by her physician.

Tim had denied the original request on the advice of the school's attorney. The district was taking the stance that the librarian could not perform the essential functions of her job and, therefore, the librarian would either need to apply for Family Medical Leave or other available leave. If she could not or would not agree to this she would need to resign due to her inability to perform the essential functions of her job as librarian.

Dr. Paulson thanked Tim for the background information on the situation and asked him to return the phone call to the reporter and keep him abreast of the situation as needed. Tim left the superintendent's office at 8:37 a.m. to tend to this and other responsibilities and assignments.

A believer in placing the right person for every position, Skip Paulson had always hired or promoted the talented individuals leading the schools and the district. His philosophy was widely known that he hired the best and then got out of their way and allowed them to become high performers. Skip Paulson was also recognized for his pragmatic approach to management and for his ability to only get intimately involved in campus and departmental affairs when absolutely necessary. This no-nonsense leadership had fostered both respect for his leadership and successful schools in the Springvale School District.

Introduction

It is a truism that many of us are cut from the same bolt of cloth when we tackle our prioritized to-do list. It seems more efficient for us to do tasks ourselves since, in our clouded mind, we figure who better to do it. We affirm, again in our mind's eye, that no one can plan, finish, and implement a project without our contributing our knowledge and wisdom along the way.

Nothing could be farther from reality for hectic school leaders. We have to learn to trust others to perform undertakings with little guidance and/or input from the principal. Trust is an easy quality for us to espouse but it is often difficult for us to let go of an important project. Our inflated egos seem to get in the way and cause us to overmanage and underlead our schools.

Self-Delusional Leadership

Consider for a moment leaders who are challenged by the false impression that they must lay a hand on every decision. Notwithstanding their altruistic goal of making certain all the wheels stay on the track, they inevitably create an organization that becomes dysfunctional. The leaders' desire to regulate decision making through strict obedience to their "hands on" practice invariably causes the school to seize up.

Hero leadership created by an organization dependent on a single title-holder is a threat to the accomplishment of the instructional vision of a school. This illusion of leadership often leads to the school organization becoming stalled when attempting to meet the instructional needs of the students.

Resulting issues surfacing in schools led by egocentric micromanagers can impact every level in the organizational hierarchy. Teachers with initiative become hesitant to implement new initiatives. Administrative staff members apprehensive of what might happen should they "go out on a limb" become indecisive decision makers. Support staff quickly learn the boss's way for performing their jobs and become automatons delivering routine service, but nothing additional. All levels defer to the micromanager for answers and decisions.

As this unfolds, employees begin to respond with a lack of enterprise and look to the boss for guidance with a "just tell me what you want me to do" mentality. Justifiably, employees lack the emotional incentive to go beyond the essence of their respective job descriptions and, as a result, carve out those responsibilities needed for survival. Lack of imagination, fear of experimentation, and loss of initiative are the legacy engendered by micromanaging school leaders.

Micromanagement versus Empowerment

Harry Chambers (2004) in his book *My Way or the Highway: The Micromanagement Survival Guide* diagnosed the issues related to working with a micromanager, noting:

> Micromangement is all about interference and disruption. It occurs when influence, involvement, and interaction begin to subtract value from people

and processes. It is the perception of inappropriate interference in someone else's activities, responsibilities, decision making, and authority. It can also be any activity that creates interference with process, policies, systems, and procedures. Basically, micromanagement is the excessive, unwanted, counterproductive interference and disruption of people and things. (14)

Unfortunately, principals of this persuasion tend to exert a direct and indirect negative impact on their school that can be devastating, as depicted in figure 4.1.

Micromanaging Principal's Impact on the School

Power Needs
The school leader who commands this type of followership is wielding an excess of positional power. True to the autocratic roots from which her leader-

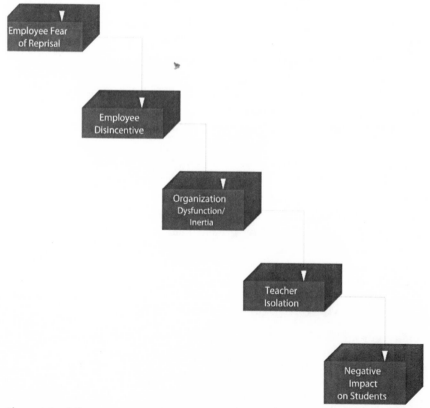

Figure 4.1. Micromanagement Impact on Teachers and Students

ship style springs, this breed of overzealous micromanager needs to command and control every situation.

Her ego is built on a base related to her position in the school's often closely guarded hierarchy. Individuals of this ilk are most likely to brandish their power on subordinates with either veiled or open threats. Intertwined with their egocentric "boss" leadership nature is a false sense that the school cannot function efficiently without their personal oversight.

Principals who control with a heavy-handedness like to control and direct the work of others like a puppeteer. Not trusting others to perform their duties without a strong measure of oversight, this form of organizational management creates a school climate reflective of the principal's "one best way" management style. Acknowledging that there are times when positional power is necessary in dealing with organizational chaos, Covey (2004) finds that one who uses his formal power as a first line of leadership builds weakness in three areas: "in self, because you are not developing moral authority; in the other, because they become codependent with your use of formal authority; and in the quality of the relationship, because authentic openness and trust never develops" (301).

All three of the areas identified by Covey are problematical for a campus. When the leader lacks ethical leadership and fails to become a servant to others the codependency cycle is exacerbated and the controlling results in the antithesis of a learning community: there is nothing to learn but the boss's way of doing things. The principal's use of positional power for decision making becomes a one-way model of control. We all recognize it as "my way or the highway" transactional thinking.

Transactional principal-leaders hold onto their power with control and coercion. Those members of their staff who fall into line are rewarded; those who "buck the system" are punished. The ensuing environment is one where employees fear reprisal knowing that "no good deed will go unpunished" under the micromanager's leadership.

While it is possible for this type of leader to be unaware that he is compromising the school's instructional program, it is highly unlikely. Most micromanagers are not mean-spirited but lack the trust necessary in the ability of others to complete tasks without an overreliance on their direction.

Impact on the Teachers and Staff

An organizational disincentive is created through micromanagement that can have negative consequences for the employees. Teachers and support staff often become disillusioned with their work causing a modicum of effort, due, in part, to their fear of unconstructive consequence should they fail to produce acceptable results.

The "organizational inertia" that follows is inextricably linked to the poor working environment created by fear or repercussions from the microman-ager's heavy-handedness. The predictable progression is for teachers and staff in these schools to self-isolate, and ultimately, student success is marginal-ized, as represented in figure 4.1.

Accountability

One of the interesting leadership aspects of micromanagers is that while they cannot or will not relinquish control, they do share accountability. If something on their watch does not show improvement—like student test scores—they are the first to blame others. The responsibility that is attached to the term *accountability*, and to the titled position of principal, can conve-niently be transferred to subordinates when academic results and other indi-cators are grim. The "blame game" that ensues is an additional contributor to the school's broken morale and teacher and staff disenchantment with the micromanager's leadership.

Visionary VAULT Leadership

The antithesis of leadership bent toward micromanagement is one that finds the principal engaged with all constituencies for school improvement. The hallmark of this type of servant leader is the trust engendered by her trans-parency and commitment to those she serves. Trusted leaders liberate their internal and external stakeholders by empowering them to be full partici-pants in the school improvement process.

Empowering others is not an abdication of the roles and responsibilities incumbent on the principalship. Schools and school leaders should carefully reflect on what it means to empower others and the attendant accountabil-ity. Starratt (1995) unveils what is meant to reflectively engage with and empower others in the school setting: "Empowerment in a school context is a relational process of surfacing what the power to be and the power to do means in this particular school, what positive qualities are attached to the ex-ercise of that power, and what limitations are imposed by the circumstances of the communal effort at schooling" (41). It is the prudent interrelation of ownership in the school's progress that results in empowerment and trust.

By engaging others in collective dialogue about school improvement, there exists a power interplay that is both healthy and acknowledging of the school's leadership capital. Creation of an expanded power base results in a talent pool that enhances the learning community's capacity to address school improvement efforts. This multifaceted alliance has at its core the improvement of teaching and learning on the campus.

Empowerment is thus seen as engaging the complementary elements of the school's collective support capital. The value added capital of culture, society, politics, nature, economic, and historical aspects become driving forces for the school improvement process. Each element contributes to the realization of agreed-upon learner-centered goals.

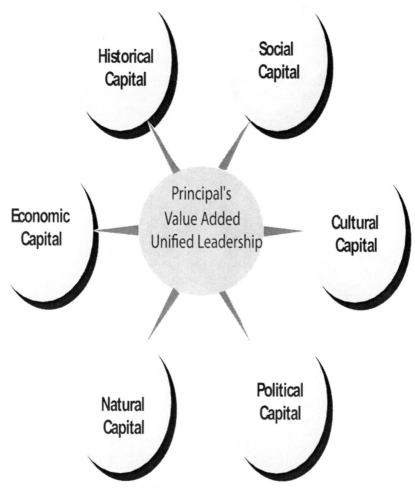

Figure 4.2. Principal's Value Added Unified Leadership

Cultural capital comprises the knowledge, skills, and dispositions of the leadership team. The team's internal and external networks provide the basis for the team's social capital. Economic capital includes the resources supporting the work of the school in concert with the historical tapestry of the school and community and their available natural resources. The interplay of these with the VAULT can be seen in figure 4.2.

Chapter Reflection

It is through an inclusive leadership perspective that schools can be stimulated to be better than they would be under a micromanager. Consider the following reflective questions:

1. Have you worked for an individual with tendencies to micromanage? If so, how did you and others in this relationship respond?
2. In this chapter's Preflection what seemed to be Skip Paulson's preferred leadership style? Did his trust of others complement the school's vision?
3. Describe three issues that come into play for a school organization when the leader is a micromanager.
4. Do you agree or disagree with the statement, "Hire the very best person for the job and then get out of the way." Why or why not?

~

CHAPTER FIVE

Building a Value Added
Unified Leadership Team

Key #4—Knowing that collaboration through distributive leadership can lead to improved academic performance through a Value Added Unified Leadership Team (VAULT) approach will lead to improved instructional support.

Preflection

The Pineview schools were beset by a flurry of concerned parents once the letter from the school's superintendent hit the street. The correspondence from Mike Chapin informed parents that a tenth grade student at one of the district's magnet schools had been diagnosed with the dreaded H1N1 flu virus. Details were sketchy but the unnamed student had recently participated in a mathematics scholar-to-scholar program hosted by a Canadian school district. His condition was unknown but he was now being quarantined as a safety measure.

Parents wanted answers and high school principal Rita Serrano was handling their questions and, at times, tantrums, in a skilled manner. Always recognized as a skillful communicator, Ms. Serrano had always been able to calm storms such as this—the community admired and trusted her judgment. This situation, however, called for her leadership and personal charisma in a uniquely challenging way.

The previous morning district administrators had been summoned to the central administrative offices for an "emergency" meeting with Dr. Chapin. Rita Serrano had been the one to inform the superintendent of

49

the student's illness. Being proactive was a principle Ms. Serrano held dear and preached to her leadership team. Now was the time to take decisive action.

Rita Serrano had immediately contacted the local health authorities as well as the district's head nurse for assistance. Once she had their input she wisely contacted the district's law firm and was put through to an attorney specializing in community health issues. Once the issues were discussed with these specialists she immediately drafted a letter to be sent out by the superintendent at the close of the previous day's classes.

Of utmost importance to Rita Serrano was student safety followed closely by the protection of the instructional day and preserving the academic focus on her campus. Knowing that the principal's time was appropriately focused on the safety issues surrounding the H1N1 flu virus, her outstanding leadership team stepped up.

Each member of the broadly defined leadership team continued to carry out the academic mission of their health sciences magnet school. Department heads, content area and technology specialists, and the school's administrative assistants joined the assistant principals by modeling academic leadership.

The leadership team was able to convey a calm presence to students and staff due to the well-designed Campus Emergency Response Plan. This detailed plan was well designed and had been updated annually by a campus advisory committee since Rita Serrano became principal four years ago. The staff knew they had created an excellent emergency plan hoping it would never have to be activated. Now they knew they had to "work the plan" as they faced this emergency.

As the key leadership met with the superintendent to decide how to proceed, the leadership team of the Pineridge High School for Heath Sciences devised a plan. Until they knew if the school would be closed or how students would be screened for the dreaded "Swine" flu, their plan would be immediately implemented.

The plan was the brain child of the veteran chemistry teacher, Stan Gillette. Since the H1N1 flu virus had now been declared a pandemic he reasoned it made sense to capitalize on the teachable moment and refocus the school's lessons to the understanding of the disease. When broached to the leadership team a small epiphany happened as members began brainstorming how they could incorporate the theme into their lesson plans. A true teachable moment emerged that would help students learn a significant and timely topic.

Introduction

Assessing the Current State of Instructional Leadership

It would seem the school organization has been mired in an early twentieth-century model forever. This feudal agrarian approach has driven education to the brink of obsolescence and yet we continue to live in the comfort of schools designed for previous generations. The current state of education reminds me of a tongue-in-cheek version of the Rip Van Winkle tale that finds Rip arising from his one hundred year sleep with the only institutions recognizable to him are the public schools.

Whether one looks at the school calendar based on the needs of an agrarian nation of a millennium ago or the "bells and cells" design of school buildings, things have not changed. Certainly the error-laden textbooks that drive a suspect curriculum in many schools are relics of the past, as is our understanding of how learning takes place.

Confounding this aged relic of bygone days we call our educational system is the way we train, hire, and utilize those in the principalship. Colleges of education continue to fall prey to political pressure to keep things as they have always been. The training of principals in most institutions uses the same outdated pedagogy that the professors rail against as they criticize P–12 education.

Identifying Gaps between the Current State and Desired State

Principal preparation programs are under fire for providing schools with a near exact replica of the school leader's position that existed in the early part of the twentieth century. The training these programs provide is often outdated, lacks rigor, and is resistant to change. Arthur Levine, president of Teachers College at Columbia University, in his much publicized criticisms of principal preparation programs has lead a chorus of individuals and organizations clamoring for change, stating, "The typical course of study for the principalship has little to do with the job of being a principal" (2005, 27).

The Southern Regional Education Board (SREB, n.d.) echoes the Levine critique of principal preparation in its publication *Schools Can't Wait: Accelerating the Redesign of University Principal Preparation Programs*. This publication describes the urgent need for the revisioning and retooling of principal preparation programs. Using data collected from universities considered to be trendsetters in the region it serves, it found that

- Current state policies and strategies intended to promote redesign of principal preparation programs have produced episodic change in a few institutions but have fallen short in producing the deeper change that would ensure all candidates master the knowledge and skills needed to be effective school leaders today.

- There is a lack of urgency for refocusing the design, content, process and outcomes of principal preparation programs based on the needs of schools and student achievement and little will happen until there are committed leaders of change at every level—state, university, and local school district.

- States and districts cannot depend on universities to change principal preparation programs on their own because the barriers to change within these organizations are too deeply entrenched.

- The issue is not whether principal preparation programs need to change, but how can states plan and carry out a redesign initiative that gets the right results? (4–5)

These criticisms are indeed a sad commentary on the preparation of the principals who are filling the position at a time of dramatic social and economic change. The world of the millennial principal is rapidly changing and the preparation programs training must keep pace.

Once the candidate completes the state's licensure requirements and assumes the principal position, little is done to continue to mentor them. The result is often principals who are both inadequately trained and poorly supported for the important work they are called upon to perform.

The gap between the role of the principal as chief academic officer of the school is often a dramatic dissimilarity with the reality of the on-the-job expectations. Principals are called upon to be everything to everyone from head of campus security to chaperone on a field trip to the museum. There continues to be a striking dissimilarity between the idealized role of the principal and the lived experience of the principal in most schools.

Considering and Implementing an Alternative:
Value Added Unified Leadership Team

We seem to know what the principal should be doing but lack the courage to reconceptualize the position to accommodate the managerial and leadership responsibilities. Many astute writers place the principal on the "leadership" side of the continuum but in actuality the role must be combined with management skills. John P. Kotter (1998), writing for the *Harvard Business Review*, advocated for viewing management and leadership as complementary functions in an organization. Kotter sees management as "coping with complexity" and leadership being "coping with change" (104).

Nurturing Leadership

Almost every approach to school reform requires principals to refocus their roles, responsibilities, and opportunities—and, as a result, to acquire new knowledge and skills. The success of efforts to increase and reach high standards depends largely on competent principals who nurture schoolwide leadership.

Hoy and Hoy (2009) affirm the importance of an instructional leader sharing the responsibilities for instruction, "Leadership in instructional matters should emerge freely from both the principal and teachers. After all, teachers deliver the instruction in the classroom; they have expertise in curriculum and teaching, and they have mastered a substantive body of knowledge. . . . Thus, principals should forge a partnership with teachers, with the primary goal of the improvement of teaching and learning" (2). The partnership between the principal and teachers in instructional matters is a crucial element for student success.

But, when carefully planned, implemented, and assessed, this partnership can expand into an alliance that more fully supports the school's instructional goals. Teacher leadership is vital but others inside and outside the school walls can richly sustain the core instructional work of principals and teachers.

This alliance could, and should, include any and all stakeholders willing to participate. Collaborators who could enhance instructional support could be tapped from the school's parents and community, the counseling department, educational support specialists, and clerical/paraprofessionals on the campus. Assistance could even come from less likely sources like the school resource officer who can assist with counseling recalcitrant students concerning the benefits of education and school completion. The array of possible candidates for the instructional improvement alliance is truly endless.

Building a Value Added Unified Leadership Team

John Kotter (1998) advocates the sharing of leadership with other talented individuals in the organization, stating, "Institutionalizing a leadership-centered culture is the ultimate act of leadership" (53). Growing leadership in others—particularly instructional leadership—will serve to create a community of learners who are empowered to support the reforms needed for twenty-first-century schools.

What we should be striving for is a balanced leadership in an era of tremendous imbalance. In a school that synergistically works in tandem to accomplish the school's goals, excellence will prevail. But this institutional renewal process requires significant planning and reflection to ensure success. The identification, mentoring, and data-driven assessment of the VAULT take a systematic development of the school's instructional talent pool.

Identifying Potential Leaders

Accomplishing this requires a strategic process that begins with the recruitment of individuals who can integrate into the community of learners yet keep their uniqueness. This step is often the one least understood and most undermanaged. It is also a critical step to get right if you are building leadership in others.

School leaders often choose expediency over due diligence with regards to staffing the school. We should remind ourselves of the parable told about the bend in the river. I'm not sure who created the tale but it speaks to us about our decision making. It goes something like this:

> The citizens of a village situated along a bend in the river noted a body floating in the water. An individual coming from upstream somewhere had obviously drowned and the body turned up on their shore. To some degree perplexed, the citizens shrugged their collective shoulders and returned to business of their town. Within days another body floated up on the shore. The citizens thought it to be a rather strange situation but, as before, returned to their daily activities. When a third body emerged at the bend in the river the elders of the village put their heads together and determined that they should build a hospital at the bend in the river to try to save the life of anyone who might be drowning in the river. Then they decided they should post a sentry at the bend in the river—one who could pull a drowning person out of the water and administer CPR before taking them to the newly erected hospital.

The obvious point to the parable is that the villagers continued to make "downstream" decisions for "upstream" problems. They never thought to look upstream for the root cause of the drowning; they were content to deal with the consequence of what was happening upstream.

The premise of this book is that individual school leaders are too busy accomplishing relatively unimportant tasks. As the tale about upstream and downstream decision making goes, we often make crucial personnel decisions without a thorough profiling of the position and selection of the very best person for the position. Steven Covey (1999), in his book *Living the 7 Habits: The Courage to Change*, reinforced this, stating,

> When you are buried by urgent matters and have a thousand balls in the air, it is easy to put people who appear to have solutions into key positions. The

tendency is to not look deeply into their background and patterns, not to do "due diligence," nor to carefully develop the criteria that needs to be met in the particular roles or assignments. I am convinced that when recruiting and selecting are done strategically, that is with long-term thought and productivity, not based on the pressures of the moment, it pays enormous long-term dividends. . . . You have to look deeply into both character and competence because eventually, downstream, flaws in either area will manifest themselves in both areas. I am convinced that although training and development are vital, recruitment and selection are even more vital. (305)

Why is it, then, that this vital fact is so imperceptible in the creation of leadership teams? It could be political pressure to bring someone on board that a board member is promoting. It could be that we are too busy to create and implement a process for building a team. It could be that we want everyone on the team to look and act like every other member and fail to look at the rich benefits of diversity. Or, as I will assume, it is because you have never really considered the importance of the recruitment and selection process for growing leaders on your campus.

To begin the selection of members for the VAULT, consider, as Covey suggests, the character and competence of both those on your staff and those you may be bringing onto the staff. Create a "profile" of the generalized knowledge, skills, and dispositions that will be meaningful selection criteria.

Robert W. Eichinger and Michael M. Lombardo (2001–2003) outline the core competencies that their research for Lominger Limited, Inc., found to be critical for serving as a principal. Their list can be a starting point for assessing the competencies needed for a school's leadership and creating a profile:

Core Competencies
Candidates who are likely to be successful in this position will demonstrate a basic grasp of the following 12 Educational Competencies. Those who will be the most successful will further demonstrate a desire to improve their skills in—and eventually master—these competencies:

- *Functional/Technical Skills*: Possesses required functional and technical knowledge and skills to do his or her job at a high level of accomplishment; demonstrates active interest and ability to enhance and apply new functional skills.
- *Motivating Others*: Creates a climate in which people want to do their best; can assess each person's strengths and use them to get the best out of him or her; promotes confidence and optimistic attitudes; is someone people like working for and with.

- *Integrity and Trust*: Is widely trusted; is seen as a direct, truthful individual; presents truthful information in an appropriate and helpful manner; keeps confidences; admits mistakes; doesn't misrepresent himself or herself for personal gain.
- *Valuing Diversity*: Manages all kinds and classes of people equitably; supports equal and fair treatment and opportunity for all; fosters a climate of inclusion, where diverse thoughts are freely shared and integrated.
- *Interpersonal Skills*: Is warm and easy to approach; builds constructive and effective relationships; uses diplomacy and tact to diffuse tense situations; has a style and charm that immediately puts others at ease and disarms hostility.
- *Managing and Measuring Work*: Clearly assigns responsibility for tasks and decisions; sets clear objectives and measures; monitors process, progress, and results; designs feedback loops into work.
- *Drive for Results*: Pursues everything with energy, drive, and a need to finish; does not give up before finishing, even in the face of resistance or setbacks; steadfastly pushes self and others for results.
- *Directing Others*: Establishes clear directions; sets stretching goals, and assigns responsibilities that bring out the best in people; establishes a good work plan and distributes the workload appropriately.
- *Managing Vision and Purpose*: Communicates a compelling and inspired vision or sense of core purpose; makes the vision sharable by everyone; can inspire and motivate entire units or organizations.
- *Priority Setting*: Spends his or her time and the time of others on what's important; focuses on the critical few, and puts the trivial many aside; can quickly sense what will help or hinder the accomplishment of a goal.
- *Decision Quality and Problem Solving*: Uses analysis, wisdom, experience, and logical methods to make good decisions and to solve difficult problems with effective solutions; appropriately incorporates multiple inputs to establish shared ownership and effective action.
- *Managerial Courage*. Tactfully dispenses direct and actionable feedback; is open and direct with others without being intimidating; deals head-on with people problems and prickly situations. (3)

Using a framework such as the desired characteristics outlined by Eichinger and Lombardo creates a starting point for assessing the leadership potential in other stakeholders.

Once you and your existing team have a sound basis for looking at others in the school organization with competencies and character you are looking for, reflect on their willingness to step forward and engage with the principal in the school's mission.

Mentoring the VAULT Alliance

As the potential talent pool is identified, it is the principal's leadership that creates the bond needed to facilitate a "unified" team. Investing in the success of your Value Added Unified Leadership Team requires effective mentoring and support. Just as one cannot expect to hire a teacher, give her a key to her room, and expect amazing results, the same is true for the leadership team. They have to be nurtured through effective mentoring and that is the principal's primary role if the VAULT is to be successful as a leadership community that positively impacts teacher growth and student learning.

School districts have for decades understood the importance of mentoring for both novice teachers and beginning principals. Mentor programs of this nature are designed to add additional support to the mix of on-the-job and university training received by these individuals.

Specific to the principalship, many P–20 school partners realize that formal preparation for the job of principal must include a practical component that can provide real-life skills through apprenticeships or internships (Malone 2001). The effectiveness of this type of training has become more important as districts confront shrinking pools of qualified candidates for both principals and mentors (Educational Research Service 2000).

According to Malone (2001), although mentoring has been around for thousands of years, it is only in the last thirty years that mentor-protégé relationships have received increasing interest. Much of this research focused on classical mentoring where the protégé found a mentor willing to serve as guide and counselor. Such mentoring tended to produce a protégé just like the mentor, which meant that issues for women and minorities were usually ignored (Samier 2000).

Principal mentoring of leadership is designed to create a lead collaborator whose chief concern is the alignment of the instructional resources for continuous improvement. As Kotter (1998) states, "What executives need to do . . . is not organize people but align them" (45). The alignment of the school's human instructional capital takes a facilitator skilled in effective communication. The leader's role is to get people to buy into the instructional vision and become believers who complement, not copy, each other.

Distributed leadership teams will face challenges as they transition into their enhanced role with the school's instructional matters. Although team members have formal university certification courses and career-based knowledge and training that provides a basic foundation for undertaking their new role, much of the guidance received comes through the instructional influence demonstrated by the instructional leader.

The professional guidance of principals as mentors is a key element for bridging the knowing-doing gap of team members and to help them grow professionally. A strong cadre of leaders will emerge over time from the administrative ranks as well as key individuals in support roles if you nurture their growth. Consider everyone that can support the school's goal attainment as leadership potential. Once identified, these individuals will need mentoring and professional development to acclimate them to the leadership community.

When the principal expands the leadership team, all participants profit from the experience with students gaining the most from the collaboration. Boreen and Niday (2003) describe mentoring as more than a relationship. It should also provide a vast array of life and professional learning experiences that enhance the ability of the mentee to interact with his or her colleagues in a collegial manner (1).

Mentoring is a process of advising, coaching, and nurturing that is focused on developing an open relationship that enhances an individual's career, and personal and professional growth and development (Young and Wright 2001). This is the essence of "value added" in nurturing leadership potential in others.

The principal's success at forging a productive mentoring relationship with members of the larger learning community will likely face challenges. Race and gender are two issues that can complicate the formation of mentor-protégé relationships. There has to be mutual respect in forging a VAULT and principals have to demonstrate to all stakeholders that they value the team's diversity regardless of the contributor's social class, gender, race, ethnicity, talents, disabilities, or religion.

Characteristics of Quality Mentor Principals
Mentors lead through example. They model the attributes and characteristics of the profession. Mentoring of the VAULT by the principal provides a model for colleagues for navigating the unpredictability of the leadership. The principal as a mentor provides a bridge that connects the VAULT's competencies and character leads to the practical application of a learning community.

Mentor principals play a crucial role in the career growth of their distributed leadership team by providing perspective-broadening insights and through their modeling of the leadership behaviors that influence and impact their educational experience and growth.

The characteristics of a mentor principal span many aspects of career, personal, and professional growth. According to Rowley (1999) these attributes include not only being skilled at providing support but also possessing effective interpersonal skills and being a model of continuous learning.

In the context of principal-as-mentor these characteristics often are not experienced in a formalized relationship with the leadership team. Rather, the VAULT is influenced through the observed actions of veteran principals as they interact with stakeholders and respond to the demands implicit in their role as leader.

The development of these individuals is inextricably connected to real-world expectations and to real-world ideals of professional leaders. As Gopalakrishnan and Hill (2009) state, "The role of leaders is to continuously create and nurture the conditions that make the exercise of leaderful behavior the everyday culture throughout the system" (4).

Assessing the VAULT's Impact

It is certainly true that we never "arrive" when we are striving for continuous instructional improvement. As the superintendent who mentored me as a principal, Dr. Gerald Anderson, often wisely told me as a high school principal eager to improve every aspect of the school at once, "John, an inch is a cinch and a yard is too hard." The wisdom I captured from this seemingly simplistic comment was that school leaders have a vision for where they want to lead a campus but it still takes time.

However, along the way we have to assess the impact of our team's success in strengthening the school's academic program. The VAULT's leadership initiatives would wisely center on a triangulation of three critical components to the change process: (1) focusing on a clear and unambiguous understanding of the past, (2) an understanding of the leverage needed to effect transformative curricular change, and (3) a thoughtful consideration of tactics required to minimize stakeholder resistance.

Understanding the Past

A school leader cannot expect to accomplish the school's goals without having a clear understanding of where the campus has been. Certainly data sources such as standardized tests tell part of the story, as does available anecdotal information. An analysis will determine if the current state—your campus's status quo—finds the financial, human, and material resources aligned to support implementation of a campus vision.

A sampling of questions the principal might consider in the role of anthropologist in gathering information about the status of your school might include:

- What are the core beliefs of the district and campus?
- How effective is the internal and external communication for the campus?

- Who in the school and community are sources of power and who has wielded their clout in the past?
- Is diversity valued?
- How are decisions made? Are they autocratic dictates or collaborative discussions? Are they data-driven and based on the evidence?
- Do the school's stated priorities and goals align with what is practiced?
- Do parents and community members feel welcome in the school?
- Are financial and/or human resources available with a significant percentage focused on instruction?
- Is hard work rewarded?
- Are there lingering unsolved issues?

Answers to these and other straightforward status questions will provide the principal with a foundation for understanding how the school's past will promote or impede his or her instructional vision. By tapping into the historical knowledge of colleagues and community members one can then create a plan of action that invites all voices into the school renewal dialogue.

Leveraging Change
A clear understanding of the past can also provide valuable information needed for honing the instructional vision and leveraging the VAULT capital mentioned in chapter 4. The historical, social, cultural, political, natural, and economic aspects of the school's culture can be directed toward successful outcomes.

Leveraging the School's Capital
Historical, social, cultural, political, natural, and economic influences are important considerations in the formulation of the VAULT's leadership assemblage but also serve as important leverage points with the broader school community. The attributes and dispositions held by a pluralism of stakeholders within the context of the school community are essential leverage points for the VAULT. We will look at each of these and examples of how the team's knowledge of what has lead to the school's status quo better prepares them to strategically execute future instructional plans.

If, for instance, your work in understanding the past has revealed a long history of racial issues, the VAULT knows that the issue of valuing diversity has to be acknowledged and built upon. Your work internally and externally must come from a place of democratic principles as you interact with various stakeholders. As Rust and Freidus (2001) explain, "[The] process of facilitating change . . . is in itself a form of discovery learning whereby new understandings are shaped by the interchange of inside and outside, and by old and new experiences and habits of the mind" (11).

As the VAULT seeks meaningful change it should tap into the cultural capital of community to bring diverse individuals and groups into the school improvement conversation. As the VAULT studies the internal and external publics they serve, they identify not only sources of power but also underrepresented groups and positions. Adding the voices of these constituent groups serves to uncover a vibrant array of support for the accomplishment of the school's mission.

Once these factions begin to invest in the school, networks are identified and democratic principles are strengthened. These opportunities for structured and nonstructured collaborative networking are vital for the VAULT and the community it serves as they grapple with complex educational issues. This process of reflexive inquiry as a community of learners manifests itself, as Richert, Stoddard, and Kass (2001) indicate, "in collaboration as people work together to make sense of their world and their experience" (139).

Additionally, identifying economic capital and the natural resources of the community requires a type of environmental scan. When the VAULT examines their community it is with an eye to creating mutually interdependent alliances. The school's reputation for educational excellence has a tremendous economic impact on the area it serves. Working together the actions of the school's economic partners can bolster the work done by teachers in the classroom. The community and its schools have a complementary relationship that serves to strengthen the education of its learners.

Conclusion

As school leaders struggle to balance their personal, professional, and spiritual lives, the more essential it becomes to rethink how we have always done things. Schools do not have the luxury to continue as an institutional vestige of the twentieth century. Teachers can't wait, parents can't wait, kids can't wait, and leaders cannot continue to operate under the old single leader paradigm.

The reality of the twenty-first century is that we are teaching millennial students who have been raised in a connected world very unlike the circumstances the human race found itself in the previous century. It is incumbent on educators to continuously think strategically about the needs of the future, not those of the past. Significant to the leadership of schools is the reconsideration of how schools operate and, in particular, how they are lead.

Chapter Reflection

Considering the challenge of the previous two paragraphs, as well as of the entire chapter, consider the Preflection in reflecting on these questions:

1. Were the schools of Pineview prepared for the event that occurred?
2. Was there evidence of collaboration in responding to the flu outbreak?
3. Was it apparent that classroom teachers felt empowered to be part of the solution?
4. Was it possible to discern the trust level of the community with the decision making of their schools?
5. How did leadership factor into the dilemma faced by the community?

CHAPTER SIX

~

Facilitating Instructional Improvement Tasks

Key #5—Knowing how to facilitate the organization of a VAULT academic improvement collaborative will assist with the structuring of instructional improvement process tasks.

Preflection

The teaching staff at McAuliffe Elementary School was beginning to implode from the demands placed on them from the "Tower." Each in his or her own way had become disillusioned from the stress of high-stakes testing, Annual Yearly Progress, and the constant barrage of parent complaints where the teacher's side is never considered.

Principal Elaine Sturgis was known for her no-nonsense, autocratic leadership style, a mode expected and supported by the superintendent of the Greenville schools. "If you can't control your campus, then get out of the way for someone with guts to do the job" was the mantra of the current administration.

Those who could find positions elsewhere had already gone, leaving those entrenched in the community, the BIGs as they were referred to: "those born in Greenville," to work in the schools. Unfortunately, the BIGs were not going to rock the boat and suffer the consequences within their tight-knit community. After all, the current superintendent was a hometown boy whose greatest claim to fame was quarterbacking the 1979 football team to a state championship.

At a tipping-point, the remaining staff had begun to take their frustrations out on the students and allow the instructional focus they had seen so richly modeled by the previous principal to fade into the town's sunset. No one desired to pick it up because they knew that "no good deed would be left unpunished" by the current administration.

As could be predicted, the school's test scores had plummeted over the course of the last four years. Where once the staff celebrated the incremental growth of student test scores and the resulting superior state accreditation ranking, a dejected staff celebrated little and were less motivated each day. Teacher absenteeism was chronic and substitutes came and went regularly.

With school trustee elections fast approaching, the superintendent was concerned for his administrative life. Out of four open positions, the three routinely elected positions were boosted by the resignation of Sandra Kerbow who resigned because of the loss of an academic focus in the district. Of the candidates running, all had the improvement of the school's academic program as their sole agenda. The community had grown weary of the district's administrative team's "my way or the highway" approach and change was in the offing.

Clearly, the community wanted change and they were not going to wait on the school board election to begin to regain their academic position. Calls for the resignation of key administrators, including the superintendent and Principal Elaine Sturgis, grew more intense as March approached.

The straw that broke the camel's back came when the superintendent supported the nonrenewal of one of McAuliffe's most outstanding teachers. Beth Roberts had been teaching only three years but had shown in that brief time an extraordinary ability to reach all of her students and positively impact their lives. It was common knowledge that she was being made an example of for her unwillingness to compromise her educational beliefs and values. She came to work each day and strived to stay above the fray but was also not one to be beaten down. The expectations she held for herself were modeled for the students in her classes and resulted in campus-leading student success.

On Friday, March 15, the notice of a special school board meeting was posted. The agenda simply stated, "Consider dismissals of administrators for cause." The vast majority of the Greenville community had finally decided it was indeed time to rock the boat and return the school district's focus to academics. They knew it would be difficult but they knew they would be looking for school leaders with strong academic credentials, good communication skills, and most importantly a plan for how to rebuild the district's academic image.

Introduction

Once a solid cadre of VAULT members has been identified, their talents need to be matched and directed toward solving the academic issues facing the school. This requires the principal to provide exemplary leadership in structuring school improvement initiatives needed for vision attainment. The approach needs to be collaborative and systematically capitalize on the VAULT's competencies and determination to provide a high-quality education for all students.

Typically, these judgments center on how to structure and match members' talents with roles and responsibilities needed for managing the instructional program. Choosing the right person for the needed function is an essential decision that must be carefully weighed. Consider aligning the known roles based on the strengths each member brings to the team. Matching his or her skills, talents, interests, and time availability to appropriate instructional assignments will avoid ambiguity and nonproductive time.

Identifying both those talents readily noticeable as well as less apparent member strengths requires reflective dialogue. A member known for being an outstanding content teacher could potentially have considerable other talents that can be utilized. For instance, a member who teaches music may also be bilingual and able to support English language learners in a content classroom or after school program. The principal's job will be to ferret out these ancillary skill sets and match them to areas of identified need. A simple self-assessment like the sample in table 6.1 might help.

The principal must encourage the VAULT to hold an unwavering value for the diversity of membership as well as the identified and latent talents each brings to the unit. Otherwise underidentified talents on a campus will remain underdeveloped unless they are brought to the surface.

Like the story of the man who sought to identify the greatest general who ever lived; he entered the Pearly Gates of heaven and asked St. Peter who the greatest general had been on earth. Thinking St. Peter would indicate someone on his list of potential candidates like MacArthur or Lee or Patton or Rommel or Marous or Hannibal or Han Xin, he was taken aback at St. Peter's response. Pointing to a disheveled woman sitting in the corner of heaven St. Peter responded that she was the most outstanding general of all time. Protesting, the man retorted, "St. Peter, I knew her when she was a mortal. She sat on the corner and asked for handouts. Surely you jest when you suggest her!" St. Peter patiently responded, "Yes, you are correct. However, had she been a general she would have been the most outstanding leader of all time."

Table 6.1. Sample Talent Survey Instrument

Prestige High School *Where Excellence Is Assured*		VAULT Talent Survey

VAULT Member Name:

Date:

Please check the talents you bring to the team in addition to your primary roles and responsibilities:

- ❑ Advocacy
- ❑ Budgeting/bookkeeping
- ❑ Community relations
- ❑ Creativity
- ❑ Database management
- ❑ Editing
- ❑ Event planning
- ❑ Fundraising/Grant writing
- ❑ Graphic design/desktop publishing
- ❑ Group facilitation
- ❑ Hospitality
- ❑ HTML support
- ❑ Foreign language (List areas of fluency):

- ❑ Newsletter publishing
- ❑ Photography
- ❑ Planning/logistics support
- ❑ PowerPoint design
- ❑ PTO
- ❑ Professional development
- ❑ Public speaking
- ❑ Publicity
- ❑ Research
- ❑ Service projects
- ❑ Site-based council
- ❑ Staff appreciation
- ❑ Website design

Other talents or skills (don't be shy):
1.
2.
3.
4.
5.

Thanks for sharing your talents

The point in the story above, which was told to me when I was a relatively new teacher, speaks volumes. The untapped and underutilized talent we fail to see in others is a resource drain on all. We have to identify and nurture the talent we see in others as well as those untouched gifts that will become value added assets for our school.

Value Added Professional Development

Developing the talents of your VAULT is essential for continuous learning and team growth. The team's growth and development is requisite for building a leadership learning community. The multitude of challenges facing twenty-first-century schools, and by extension the VAULT's work, make continued professional development imperative.

The challenges schools face, both known and unknown, requires a vigilant pursuit of knowledge and skills to close the team's knowing-doing gap. Changing demographics, demands for reform, and the need to master new proficiencies place added emphasis to the need for high-quality team development. Fullan (1995) supporting the crucial need for continued growth states, "The key to enacting moral purpose is 'continuous learning' which is another way of saying that continuous professional development is essential" (255).

High-quality professional growth is not only the structured and focused trainings that typically center on one topic but also should include a variety of opportunities to grow through professional organizations: webinars, list serves, or simply dialoguing with colleagues on pedagogical issues critical to the profession. All purposeful venues should be available for members of the VAULT.

These opportunities secure the relevance needed for success with the reforms the school is implementing through the VAULT's leadership. Educational change, and particularly as it relates to professional development, must begin with a focus on the teaching-learning process at the classroom level. Professional development should be focused on supporting teachers and their needs for providing an excellent and equitable instruction for all students. As the leadership team's knowledge and skills become translated into the school's classrooms, their status as instructional leaders will be enhanced.

Value Added Instructional Planning
Professional development not only strengthens the VAULT's instructional competence it also adds to the staff's confidence in their curricular leadership. Gaining this trust requires the leadership to plan for instruction in a seamless progression leading to fulfillment of the commonly held vision.

Translating the vision into an instructional process is a challenge of a significantly larger magnitude than simple day-to-day management. One can liken it to the difference in planning a trip to the grocery store as opposed to taking a lengthy vacation. The first takes a well-conceived shopping list, a sure car, and your ever-ready credit card, all of which takes a modicum of planning. The latter takes considerable planning. Vacations take the same steps as going to the grocery store but additional thought must be given to lodging, research on attractions along the way, and mapping.

Distributed Ownership of Results (DOOR)

VAULT DOOR

Opening the DOOR to the VAULT requires not only effective selection of members and their professional development but also the need to assess their work. Planning for instructional effectiveness using the VAULT approach requires significant "mapping" and sometimes rerouting the work to constructively navigate the challenges of school reform.

The VAULT's mapping of their tasks and responsibilities must be focused on student-related outcomes. The principal is responsible for articulating the school's vision—its preferred future state—in a process that is aligned with the school's values, mission, and goals and includes representation from all stakeholders.

As Shaver (2004) states, "The leader will be instrumental in guiding this discussion to ensure the identified outcomes are in line with building and district expectations and needs" (96). Additionally, the work needs to be indexed on state and national standards with clear, unambiguous, referent points for determining progress. It is imperative that the principal collaboratively leads the mapping of the instructional terrain to focus on what students learn and teachers need to do to meet their learning needs.

Profile of a Graduate

This process begins by idealizing the profile of what a graduate from the district's schools should look like. This is done by identifying the knowledge, skills, and dispositions needed by the graduate to be a productive citizen in our democracy. It is imperative that the VAULT and its community of learners can visualize the school's output, its graduates.

Profiling the Knowledge Base

A well-educated graduate will provide a starting point for discussing what the expectations are for students at the end of their P–12 school experience. As an example, the district may feel the graduate should be expected to emerge as an "educated person of integrity, thoroughly knowledgeable in the core curriculum and capable of analytical reasoning." Whatever the profile of the graduate's knowledge, it identifies what the graduate should be able to do as a result of his or her school experience.

Profiling of the Skills

The district needs a clear understanding of the skill sets their graduates will need as they exit. Certainly, a well-prepared graduate in the twenty-first century needs a very different set of skills to lead a productive life compared with past generations. Although, as was mentioned in an earlier chapter, we are living in the Millennial generation, many schools still exhibit expectations that, at best, are based on skills reflective of the Industrial generation.

The profile of valued skills needs to recognize and revision the graduate's personal and work-related proficiencies due to globalization. As an example, the current generation will be expected to be skillful with mobile tools such as cell devices operating on 4G networks, 2-D bar-coding devices, PDAs, Twitter, and global positioning systems (GPS). The skills of yesteryear are obsolete and current and future graduates will be handicapped in their personal and work lives by agrarian skill sets.

Profiling of the Dispositions
As citizens of a democracy we need to produce graduates who are fruitful participants in the American democratic experience. A profile of these dispositions would include the values held by the school community.

Certainly chief among these would be the graduate's demonstration of democratic values and responsible citizenship. As Jenlink (2009) states, "Democratic education, then, is linked to freedom, to the ability to see and also to alter, to understand and also re-create, to know and also imagine a world of education different from the one we have inherited, so as to provide a stronger, more viable democracy through a stronger, more democratic education for the children of today and tomorrow" (10). This ideal should be a disposition expectation for all graduates.

Opening the DOOR: Mapping for Success
Once the visioning process has produced the profile of a graduate we need a roadmap to plan and assess the progress we are making toward achieving that ideal. As the saying goes, we have to plan the work and work the plan.

Planning and the assessment of the school's progress are management tools needed for systematically identifying what is going well. Additionally, this process will uncover gaps that exist in goal attainment from the review of formative and summative data. As John Dewey (1938/1972) wisely states,

> An idea then becomes a plan in and for the activity to be carried out. Suppose a man has a desire to secure a new home, say by building a house. No matter how strong his desire, it cannot be directly executed. The man must form an idea of what kind of house he wants, including the number and arrangement of rooms, etc. He has to draw the plan, and have blue prints and specifications made. All this might be an idle amusement for spare time unless he also takes

stock of his resources. . . . But they have to be viewed and judged in order that a desire may be converted into a purpose and a purpose into a plan of action. (69–70)

Planning for instructional improvement is designed to do just what Dewey suggests, turn the profile of our graduate into a plan of action that can positively impact his or her success in life.

Familiar as a tool for curriculum implementation and assessment, mapping can also be utilized in the context of assessing the work of the distributed leadership team. Mapping, of course, is a metaphor for organizing the work that needs to be done—in this case, the important instructional leadership work.

This step-by-step "opening of the VAULT DOOR" provides the map for the school's instructional tasks, task responsibilities, data-driven assessment strategies, effective communication of results, and a date certain benchmarking timeline. The intended results can then be compared to the realized benchmark data for continuous fine-tuning by the VAULT. Distributed ownership of results (DOOR) is thus attained.

VAULT Action Mapping

Each step in the design of the action mapping tool is central to the distributed leadership team's progress toward meeting the school's goals. This connectivity will provide a bond among team members and keep each person abreast of the work being done, actions needing modification, and the issues still to be addressed.

The mapping of distributed leadership tasks includes seven important steps: (1) collection of data, (2) VAULT gap analysis of disaggregated data, (3) teacher review of disaggregated data, (4) schoolwide review of disaggregated data and reflective dialogue on gaps, (5) intermediate redirection of human and financial resources based on gap analysis, (6) identification of long-term actionable gaps, and (7) continuous improvement assessment and revision. The continuous improvement planning process can be visualized in figure 6.2. The process is essentially a goal-setting tool with the goals predicated on the available data. Data become the evidence the VAULT needs for identifying the primary and secondary challenges facing the school. It will also identify critical issues that impact the relative success of the stated goals.

Looking closer at the steps identified in mapping leadership team tasks will reveal the substantive essence of the process. Packaged together these realizations will lead to a collaborative dialogue focused on continuous improvement

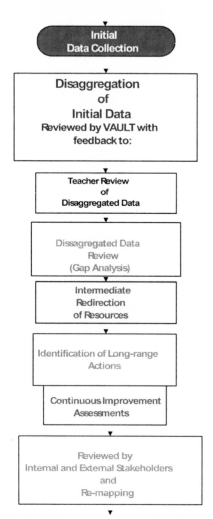

Student Learning Expectations
(Knowledge and Skills Outcomes)

**Initial
Data Collection**

**Disaggregation
of
Initial Data**
Reviewed by VAULT with
feedback to:

**Teacher Review
of
Disaggregated Data**

Disaggregated Data
Review
(Gap Analysis)

Intermediate
Redirection
of Resources

Identification of Long-range
Actions

Continuous Improvement
Assessments

Reviewed by
Internal and External Stakeholders
and
Re-mapping

Collect student & departmental/grade level data
Generate appropriate reports & distribute to relevant
decision-making groups
Based on the assessment data, make improvements
Share with external stakeholders

Figure 6.1. Continuous Improvement Planning Process

that identifies the tasks necessary for championing the school's instructional goals.

A team process systematically overseen by the VAULT is indispensable in order to do justice to the immense amount of data available to schools. Gutherie and Schuermann (2010) point out the importance of the analysis of data being lead by a team,

> One important support is a data leadership team. A team, rather than an in-dividual, is ideally suited for this work for a number of reasons. To begin with, principals and other school leaders have been given a difficult charge: take an abundance of student and demographic data, provided from a variety of sources and in various formats, and turn these data into targeted information that can be used to enhance educational practice. The sheer magnitude of this task would make it difficult for even a "superhero" principal to single-handedly accomplish. (268)

The main premise of this book as well as this chapter reaffirms the need to distribute the many roles and responsibilities of the principal, including the task of data collection, analysis, and utilization.

Collection of Data

Data are the life blood of continuous improvement. School leaders should examine multiple sources of information to begin their instructional as-sessment. The information gleaned from the school's self-examination is what Gordon Cawelti, writing in the foreword to *Indicators of School Quality* (Fitzpatrick 2002), found helped stakeholders "examine how they are doing on the critical factors that help ensure that all students attain high levels of achievement" (x). This is the VAULT's first, and most important, step.

Valuable data will come from both internal and external sources. Repre-sentative of prospective internal sources would include standardized tests, benchmark test results, grade distributions and failure rates, student and staff demographic information, drop out information, climate surveys, and local data. External data can come from state, national, and/or interna-tional assessments, parent and community surveys, employer surveys and feedback, and the school's graduate follow-up surveys. In either case, all data analysis needs to be directed toward positively impacting student suc-cess and equity.

VAULT Gap Analysis of Disaggregated Data

Data provided from the sources mentioned above becomes the evidence needed to make sound judgments about programs, content areas, teachers, and individual students. In reviewing the data the VAULT needs to view the big picture first, followed by its disaggregation. The big picture view provides the teams with overarching impressions but it is not until the data is analyzed through disaggregation that a complete understanding can be elicited and trends emerge that can be shared with teachers.

Disaggregated data are one of the most powerful descriptors of your school's progress toward educational excellence and equity. Data "mined" through the disaggregation process more fully provides the VAULT with diagnostic information and a means for interpreting the school's status. Data are typically disaggregated for gender, race/ethnicity, and socioeconomic groups.

A school's finely discriminated data will tell the VAULT what programs and initiatives are working and those that need to be addressed. An early proponent of disaggregating student data, effective schools researcher Lawrence W. Lezotte with JoAnn Cipriano Pepperl (1999) sum up data's importance to school improvement, stating,

> Disaggregation is a very powerful tool that can help you find and frame the problems in a school. What it does, more than anything else, is to force people to stop looking simply at processes and start looking at results or outcomes.
>
> Each school has to look at itself in context. Take the time to look at the data and get indicators. When you start to pull this together, remember the goal. We're trying to answer the question of who's profiting, and by how much, through our current programs of curriculum and instruction. Once we answer that question, we can identify our problem areas and develop our plans for improvement. (97)

Once the school's data is reviewed and organized by the VAULT it must be shared with teachers—those impacting the students the most.

Teacher Review of Disaggregated Data

Individual teachers, as well as content compatible groups, should be looking at the trend data distilled by the VAULT to diagnose problem areas, design remedial measures when needed, and identify needed professional development. Teachers are experts at diagnosing instructional issues and will appreciate a systematic process where a substantial amount of the disaggregation and preliminary analysis has been completed by the leadership team.

Once these data are shared, teachers can begin to use the analysis to diagnose at the classroom level, look for performance gaps with identified populations and individual students, implement remedial strategies, and continue to reassess progress. These discussions are not one-size-fits-all.

The data paints a picture of what may be happening at the classroom level, with the dynamics of the data playing out quite differently from teacher to teacher, classroom to classroom, and with individual learners. As Gutherie and Schuermann (2010) conceive, "Data vary in purpose, frequency, type of feedback provided and targeted audience" (271). DiPaola and Hoy (2008) echo this, stating, "Because students, their teachers, and classrooms are so different, the mechanics of identifying discrepancies must be flexible" (121).

Schoolwide Review of Disaggregated Data and Reflective Dialogue on Gaps

As was pointed out earlier in the chapter, the principal needs to be not only the lead learner but also the lead facilitator of the school improvement dialogue. She or he needs to be armed with essential questions that will stimulate the discussion and brainstorming of ideas. Questions like: How will our kids be impacted by the implementation of this reform (or strategy)? How will we know we are successfully implementing the reform (or strategy)? or, How will we know our kids are truly engaged in their learning (or strategy)?

Leaders who lead schoolwide discussions of this nature win from at least three points of view. First, they are seen as instructional leaders who are passionate about student success and equity. Second, they develop teachers' autonomy as they share responsibility for setting the school's direction. And finally, the community, parents, and students understand that education is a priority and join the "village" that supports their schools. Fullan (2001) draws this conclusion about knowledge sharing, "Effective leaders understand the value and role of knowledge creation, they make it a priority and set about establishing and reinforcing habits of knowledge exchange among organizational members" (87).

Changing the dialogue on a campus from what is best for teachers to what is best for students is a leadership challenge. Reflective dialogue looks to the past for what worked and what did not as well as to the future for advancing teaching and learning through problem solving.

Intermediate Redirection of Human and Financial Resources Based on Gap Analysis

Data mining and data sharing are crucial steps to the VAULT; however, a pragmatic process for considering the challenges to address and those that the school, realistically cannot immediately address is required. There are a multitude of tools to assist VAULT members in determining what is possible considering the available financial and human assets.

Some models are borrowed from economics and the business world and may have limited value for the VAULT. One model that bears mentioning is the CIPP model developed by Stufflebeam in 1966 and modified and improved to a recent (2002) iteration. CIPP is an acronym standing for the elements necessary for evaluating the context (C), input (I), process (P), and products (P) of an organization.

These four elements are designed to have stakeholders ask, What needs to be done? How should it be done? Is it being done? Did it succeed? (3). School leaders can adapt this model to continually assess the progress being made to improve instructional programs on their campus.

By looking at the data with an evaluation model like CIPP, school leaders can determine the financial and human resources needed to close identified gaps. Identified needs can be more easily supported in the budgetary process when supported by indisputable data.

Identification of Long-Term Actionable Gaps

Gaps in the school's expected performance and its realized performance based on the evidence gleaned from internal and external data sources, as well as individual classrooms, must be considered in context. For instance, a teacher in a special needs classroom should be considered within the context of her assignment, as opposed to a teacher in a gifted/talented setting. Similarly, schools in high-poverty areas should be viewed in a different context than a high-wealth school.

Let me be clear, this does not mean lower expectations for one group over another. It does mean that a different allocation of human and financial resources might be needed to support an equitable education for all campuses/classrooms.

Gap analysis follows a relatively simple flow and identifies differences between the projected or desired goal and the data evidence. The Charles A. Dana Center (2004) at the University of Texas codified the process steps for schools developing improvement plans:

1. Lay the groundwork for this process by explaining that identifying gaps does not mean that individuals are at fault. Rather it is a means of examining systemic factors that contributed to the current state.
2. Using the scale to determine the current state is most successful if the group doing this work is assured that they can be honest in their assessments without fear of retribution. One way to reinforce this is to have participants write their ratings on stickies that are collected and posted

on a flip with a scale drawn on it. This will support anonymity. The evidence that is given to support ratings is usually delivered verbally, but it could be written and collected in an anonymous process if the leader knows that individuals have concerns.

3. The information gathered in this process needs to be written up and reviewed by the team that is working on the improvement plan. If questions arise from this review process, the team could outline a means of investigating the issue to verify it.

4. The intent of this process is to gather information that will be used to develop a future or desired state based on the indicators that are on the gap analysis worksheet. The team may decide to write additional indicators or to revise existing indicators if it decides that the need exists.

5. As a result of identifying the gaps between the current state and the future state, planning teams can develop a problem statement that summarizes the underlying structural issue that needs to be addressed. A root cause analysis can then be developed in order to determine the factors that are crucial to improvement.

6. The factors that are identified are then used in the development of goals and objectives for the improvement plan. (2–7)

It is the final step in the Dana Center's process that addresses the "actionable" gaps. Identified needs can then be projected into the campus budget.

Continuous Improvement Assessment and Revision
The actionable gaps identified in the steps above can be filtered through a decision mechanism to determine the causal factors and strategize possible solutions for the identified issue. Models abound and should be matched to the complexity of the situation as well as the decision makers' expertise, competence, and commitment.

One model easily adapted for use in working with the VAULT and classroom teachers is proffered by Hoy and Tarter (1995). This model uses a seven-step decision-making cycle:

1. Define the problem.
2. Diagnose the problem.
3. Develop alternatives.
4. Consider the consequences.
5. Evaluate alternatives.
6. Select an action strategy.
7. Implement the strategy. (142)

Taking the seven-step cycle outlined above and reducing it to five, VAULT leaders, along with targeted groups of teachers, can assess the impact for modifications to programs, initiatives, strategies, and lessons. The refined five-step cycle becomes (1) define the problem identified through data disaggregation evidence; (2) diagnose the problem identified through data disaggregation evidence; (3) develop alternative practices based on instructional experience, expertise, and innovation; (4) consider the strengths, weaknesses, opportunities, and threats (SWOT) of alternative(s); and (5) implement the alternatives that will have the most impact on student success.

Defining the Problem Identified through Data Disaggregation Evidence
The first step in the decision-making process is to accurately define the identified gap. This is the most important phase of the decision-making cycle. The data leadership team should clearly define the parameters of the problem. An example would be, "Our male fourth grade students are consistently performing below that of the females in science on a standardized measure." A word of caution: teachers need to feel supported and that the principal and VAULT are not assessing blame but rather working collaboratively on the challenge facing the school or classroom.

Diagnosing the Problem Identified through Data Disaggregation Evidence
The campus data team has identified the gap between where you are and where you want to be. Once the problem is in focus it is time to begin the diagnosis. Start by gathering all the data evidence available and begin to diagnose the causes. By reflecting on the data, the VAULT can begin to look for patterns, themes, or trends that may emerge.

Using the example from the first step above, the data may reveal that this has been a trend for several years and never uncovered or discussed. This awareness will lead to a dialogue on scientifically based best practices for motivating and engaging males in the science classroom. This step will take time and the leadership team is cautioned to remain positive and refrain from assigning culpability or foisting their "solutions" on the teachers involved.

Developing Alternative Practices Based On
Instructional Experience, Expertise, and Innovation
Everyone involved brings a wealth of instructional knowledge to the table based on experiences with "what works" and what does not. Tap into the collective wisdom of the VAULT and teachers by brainstorming possible alternative best practices as your team considers the evidence discussed in the diagnosis stage.

Although it is not mandatory that the diagnosis leads to consensus, the team should be able to pinpoint strategies and interventions that are possible solutions. Just the nature of brainstorming entails participants' valuing the ideas and solutions suggested by others. School improvement dialogue based on courtesy, respect, and professionalism will evolve into empowered teachers.

Consider the Strengths, Weaknesses, Opportunities, and Threats (SWOT) of Alternatives

Strategies developed from the conversations about the school's data evidence will, through the process steps above, gel into viable alternatives to close the existing gaps. Once the team has dissected the data and found potential solutions we have to know whether the instructional alternative(s) selected are feasible. This requires a process for determining the constraints their alternative could face during implementation.

One way to move the team through this stage is to use the familiar SWOT method. This method is easy to use and asks at each of the four sectors, What are the strengths of this alternative? What are the weaknesses of this alternative? What opportunities are present with this alternative for impacting the instructional gap? and, What threats might surface that will work against the alternative's success? You will find teachers to be very excited to have the opportunity to more fully explore the alternative chosen.

In addition to going into the implementation with their collective eyes wide open, this process will engender teachers' ownership for the selected practice. As Porter et al. (2000) found in a three-year study of professional development:

> Activities with greater collective participation of teachers also tended to place more emphasis on content, provide more opportunities for active learning, and offered more coherent professional development than other activities. In turn, professional development that was content-focused and coherent and had active learning was more successful in improving teacher knowledge and eliciting changes in teachers' classroom practices. (6)

Clearly, participation by teachers in dialogue about their own practice has a direct positive impact on the students they teach. Corcoran (1995) affirms this and advocates that teachers "need to deepen their content knowledge and learn new methods of teaching. They need more time with colleagues . . . to revise the curriculum. They need opportunities to develop, master and reflect on new approaches to working with children" (2).

Implement the Alternatives That Will Have the Most Impact on Student Success
It is clear that most plans break down at the implementation stage, even
well-thought-out planning like the steps above. This does not have to be the
case if the VAULT is committed to following through as the practice is put
into place at the classroom level.

For teachers to integrate best practices into their classroom they must be
supported. Too often we expose teachers to a strategy and assume they will
not need additional support. It is imperative that VAULT members are visible in classrooms and viewed by teachers as supporting them as they refine
their practice. By visiting classrooms, principals, distributed leadership team
members, as well as peer teachers enhance the efforts at closing identified
instructional gaps.

The success of this process is evaluated ultimately on the basis of its impact on teacher effectiveness and student learning through the continual
assessment of future data evidence. As Darling-Hammond and McLaughlin
recommend, "Teachers need to be able to analyze and reflect on their practice, assess the effects of their teaching, and then refine and improve their
instruction" (1995, 93).

Chapter Reflection

In the Preflection we found the teaching staff at McAuliffe Elementary
School in near revolt against the district's loss of its instructional focus.
When a school or a district has at its core a misplaced value, the entire culture becomes tainted. The natural progression of this downward spiral is a
strong negative impact on the instructional program and, thusly, the students
they serve. The resulting school culture is one that has lost the core purpose
of providing a high-quality education to every child.

Sergiovanni (2009) discusses how schools led by purposeful school leaders
are advantaged over those with a lost perspective,

> Purposing is a key characteristic found by others who have studied success-
> ful schools in the United States. This research establishes the importance of
> shared goals and expectation and approved modes of operation that create a
> strong school culture. Important to this culture are the norms and values that
> provide a cohesion and identity and that create a unifying moral order from
> which teachers and students derive direction, meaning and significance. (182)

Schools with leaders who exhibit a vision crystallized and centered on democratic values position their students for success.

The principal's leadership in forming purposeful alliances designed to improve the teaching and learning process has never been as important. In the age of just-in-time delivery of goods and the proliferation of technology, schools can no longer dig themselves into the rituals of the past and expect to achieve greatness.

Classroom teachers are the heart of the school and school leaders must value both their ability to review data, diagnose instructional concerns, and choose appropriate interventions for their students. Schools that collaborate in finding solutions to complex curricular and instructional challenges become powerful instructional advocates for kids.

1. Reflecting on the dilemma of McAuliffe Elementary School, how could disaggregated data support the teachers' desire to see instructional improvements?
2. How can reflective dialogue among the learning community improve the delivery of a high-quality education?
3. What part does vision and purpose play in the school improvement process?
4. How are students in today's schools different than in previous generations? How can schools utilize technology to improve instructional strategies?
5. High-quality professional development is a key to improved classroom practice. As a school leader how would you leverage these opportunities to maximize their impact on instruction?

CHAPTER SEVEN

~

Motivating Instructional Improvement

Key #6—Knowing that a motivated self leads to motivated others in the organization will invigorate the school with students becoming the academic beneficiaries.

Preflection

Veteran principal Cynthia Ann Teasdale was feeling she was in a downward spiral. Acknowledged for her curriculum credentials and a firm commitment to serving all kids, she felt her energy level was sapped as she tried to pay attention to the speaker at the district's beginning of the year convocation.

Racing through her mind were all the start-up issues still to be done: student schedules, new teacher orientation, and finalization of innumerable other issues from the lunch schedule to the implementation of the new AP World History course. Playing like a movie being fast-forwarded, her to-do list was on a continuous loop through her mind.

Just as she began to have the same anxiety attack she experienced every year at this point she returned to the comments being made by Stu Hughes, a nationally recognized motivational speaker. Something he said about Noah caught her attention and she began to refocus on the comments of the speaker.

Stu Hughes was using the metaphor of Noah's Ark to make his comments to the faculty and staff at their beginning of the year convocation. Hughes would situate each of the truisms in a school-related context and described for his audience how they could make small changes in their personal and professional lives and increase both their productivity and personal vigor.

"Don't miss the boat"; "Don't forget we're all in the same boat"; "Plan ahead. It wasn't raining when Noah built the ark"; "Stay fit. When you're 600 years old someone might ask you to do something really big"; "Don't listen to critics; just get on with what has to be done"; and "For safety's sake, travel in pairs" were the six points Stu Hughes shared along with their application to the teaching-learning audience. He was a skillful presenter with his appearance designed to energize those in attendance and begin the school year on a highly motivated note.

Cynthia Ann Teasdale had heard many speakers over her thirty-plus years in education and nineteen years as a campus administrator. She could certainly find value with all of the items on Stu's list but something about the "Stay fit. When you're 600 years old someone might ask you to do something really big" point hit home.

Reflecting, Cynthia noted to herself that over the last seven years as a high school principal she had gained twenty-five pounds, had stopped playing tennis, and eliminated all forms of exercise from her daily routine. She also made a mental note that her eating habits had deteriorated to her skipping breakfast, eating little for lunch, and when she could be home in the evenings resorting to grabbing fast food to take home.

All of these decisions, Cynthia Ann realized, were unconsciously made to save time for tending to school-related tasks. The speaker's comments resonated with her and she realized that she had to keep fit in all aspects of her life if she was to be the leader she knew she could, and should, be. It would become a campus priority for her to resurrect the campus's wellness program and encourage her staff by her active participation in these activities. She knew just the person on the school's faculty she would ask to assist her in the new faculty and staff wellness program.

Introduction

Team building is essential to effect success on a campus. The synergy that develops when principals take the lead in developing talent and motivating employees is essential to the school's progress toward meeting its goals. Principals are called upon to consider their commitment, not only to the attainment of the school's goals, but also to how goal setting can be a tremendous motivator for building collegiality. In order to energize the staff and students, the principal and leadership team have to set both organizational and personal stretch goals.

As has been said, if the leader turns around and no one is following, then the leader is not leading. Sergiovanni (2009) suggests that a leader of others has to also become a follower, "The successful leader . . . is one who builds up the leadership of others and who strives to be a leader of leaders. A successful leader is also a good follower—one who follows ideas, values, and beliefs" (184). The structuring of a community of learners, each passionate about results rather than personal recognition, requires an understanding of one's self and goal-attainment strategies that motivate others toward the accomplishment of the leader's vision for high performance.

School improvement, as represented in figure 7.1, is a process founded on the leader's vision for the school. Enmeshed in the vision are the core beliefs held by both the school's stakeholders and the leader. Converting the abstract concepts of vision and beliefs into a viable improvement plan for the campus requires concrete goal setting and action planning in an inclusive approach. Results are monitored and goals are then revised in a systematic and evolutionary analysis process. The leader's work is to make certain the plan is clearly communicated, actualized, and the results evaluated in accordance with all available data.

Getting Started: Vision and Beliefs

How does the leader realize the vision of educational excellence that has a positive impact on student success and equity and, at the same time, remain motivated? The answer is found in the goal setting process that can become a self-fulfilling prophesy. The more the VAULT leadership and staff *believe* they can accomplish campus goals, the more they will *try* to accomplish the goals, and the more successful they *will* be in goal attainment.

This process begins with the leader's vision of what schools can, and should, look like. If the leadership couples their vision of what is possible with a recognizable belief system, the campus will be motivated to do whatever it takes to reach every child, every day, everywhere they encounter them.

Visioning the Future

Your school's improvement journey starts with the principal as he challenges the status quo with beliefs based on a crystal-clear vision for the campus as a community of learners and an understanding of his critical role in leading needed change efforts. Democratic principal-leaders who understand their schools as learning organizations share a common set of beliefs and position others to achieve organizational goals.

Keefe and Jenkins point to three characteristics that facilitate schools being successful: (1) well-developed core competencies, (2) attitudes supportive of continuous improvement, and (3) the capability to redesign and renew the processes of the organization (1997, 3).

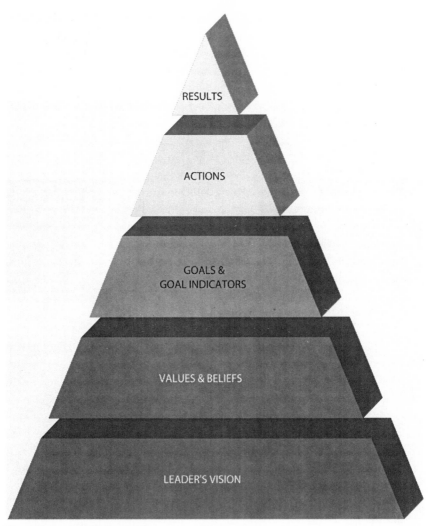

Figure 7.1. Results Pyramid

Keefe and Jenkins' work expanded their definition of core competencies to include the administration of the school's personnel policies and practices, its program of professional development, and the delivery of instruction. Supportive attitudes centered on a culture of continuous improvement based on the institutional norms and high expectations in providing a "challenging curriculum, authentic instruction and assessment, and good communication." In regards to the capability for the organization to renew itself, the authors pointed to the need to foster a commitment to "intellectual quality, school community, and sustained effort" that is flexible in responding to environmental demands (3).

These beliefs provide a foundation for visioning a preferred future for each child in the leader's school. Translating the core competencies into a viable vision, according to Cunningham and Cordeiro (2009), requires the leader to take interrelated "ideas, knowledge, experience, and futurist thinking" and translate them into a framework of goals. This reflective step codifies the visionary leader's core beliefs into goals that can be communicated to stakeholders and put into an action plan.

Goal Setting

Preface

Readers are probably musing, "Here we go again, another rehashing of goal setting steps of which I am very well versed; thank you very much!" I actually totally agree: school leaders do know the process for setting schoolwide goals. Unfortunately, this is another example of a knowing-doing gap.

We do know how to set goals at a knowledge level; it is at the follow-through level where great planning is often negated for otherwise sound school goals. It is the actions we take, or conversely fail to take, that causes what I term "goal mold." The goal setting plan is put in order then put on the shelf to gather dust until the next go around the following year. The breakdown is at both the implementation stage as well as the formative and summative assessment stages in a school's goal setting process.

Full Stakeholder Participation

Effective goal setting is a process and one that should be as inclusive as possible. Schools, as open systems, are interdependent with parents, families, their community, and other state and national forces (Stanford 1998, 60). Schools should recognize that parents and the community are not "constituents"—they are partners with a tremendous stake in what the schools do for their children and the community they serve. We, as educators, need to do "whatever it takes" to provide a supportive bridge to our parents and community members and involve them in the academic lives of their children.

One way to do this is to genuinely involve parents and the community in the ongoing process of goal setting. The resulting alliance promotes improved understanding that, in turn, strengthens the school's cultural capital as parents and the community become full partners alongside educators in their school's continuous improvement process.

It is incumbent on the school and its leadership to reach out to parents and the community in a meaningful relationship. With dramatic shifts in demographics in twenty-first-century schools, this means utilizing multiple communication means to make contact and sustain stakeholder involvement. As full partners, parents and the community must be made to feel valued and their ideas for improving schools worthwhile. This outreach is an ongoing process that must be situated in trust and the maintenance of mutual respect for the contributions of all participants.

Goal Attainment Process

Turning the school's vision into a reality requires a methodical approach that is centered on the student success and equity as mentioned previously. Schools too often are organized around what's best for the staff with processes—including goal setting—focused on making the "work" environment comfortable for them. The first step for school leaders in effective goal setting within the school organization has to be to turn this around to focus on what's best for the kids we are here to serve.

The reality is that this concept generally gets the appropriate level of lip service support from the staff, followed closely by the campus returning to making it more about comfort zones and maintaining the status quo than about student success and equity. Although recognizing that not all individuals will become instant adopters of the principal's vision, this is a time when the leader really has to show the way through words and actions. As Paul B. Thornton writes in his book *Be the Leader: Make the Difference* (1999), "When you see people stuck in their comfort zones—in their thinking, attitudes, or behaviors—you need to step forward as a leader and provide a challenge" (9).

Miner (2005) writing on motivation studies conducted by Kurt Lewin indicates that three factors influence the setting of organizational goals: "the seeking of success, the avoiding of failure, and a cognitive factor representing a probability judgment" (43). In other words, principals need to recognize that staff members' confidence that goals can be attained, or conversely their fear of goal failure, is based on their experiences and the learned "probability" for success or failure. The old adage that success breeds success is appropriately true when motivating staff to set high expectations through the campus goals setting process.

Goals: The Long and the Short of It

What constitutes a goal being long-term as opposed to short-term is a tricky subject. As Bluedorn and Ferris report (2004), in America "time capsules are intended to be opened in one hundred years" as opposed to the time orientation within the Japanese culture where "some time capsules specify they are to be opened in five thousand [years]" (114). In most school districts we find strategic planning to be the long-range goal setting window and typically be for a five- to ten-year period.

At the campus level, planning usually is characteristically patterned on a year-to-year time frame and constitutes short-term horizons that encompass a specific academic school year. This can be problematical for the visionary school leader from two perspectives. First, leading in this short-term environment requires the principal to continually revisit with teachers and other stakeholders the goals that have been set for the current school year and their progress toward their realization. Second, an effective school leader must keep the staff's focus on the long-range goals that undergird the campus vision.

Simply put, even though the campus sets long-range stretch goals, the staff and stakeholders serving the campus must believe the goals they produced are achievable. Based on the data available to planners the team must set short-range targets that, while still stretching toward the vision, provide incremental benchmarks for monitoring progress.

These steps serve to mitigate feelings that can surface when staff members do not view the goal setting process as meaningful based on their prior experiences with unrealistic expectations. Their learned fear of failure, or fear of being held tightly accountable, can easily derail the goal setting process. As one of Lewin's experiments bore out, employees are more comfortable with stretch goals when they are broken into a series of short-range goals they feel are doable (Miner 2005, 43).

Another challenge faced by school leaders is that sound, systematic campus improvement planning must be indexed to the budget to be sure needed resources are available. Too often these two elements are handled separately, leaving the campus to "shoot in the dark" at school improvement targets that require innovative approaches and funding. This situation is often the result of an impractical state funding mechanism usually created a biennium at a time. To offset this, principals must work within the existing school goal setting process by working with stakeholders to prioritize the *needs* from the *wants* and the *must haves* from the *nice to haves*.

Prioritization of Campus Goals
The process of prioritizing is the leader's first step in communicating the work that is vital on the campus. As Covey, Merrill, and Merrill (1994) state, "This process [prioritization] enables you to translate your personal mission

statement into the fabric of your daily life. From the mission to the moment, it empowers you to live with integrity and put first things first in a balanced, principle-centered way" (78). Taken to the organizational level, prioritization gives emphasis to the important goals and action steps within the very complex world of education.

The process of prioritization is one of communication: communication with all levels of the internal organization's hierarchy, as well as in the "open" educational organization with parents, community, and partners. The leader must communicate with, not to, others in the organizational structure by asking questions and seeking input, as Hochheiser (1998) wisely suggests, "not in a way as to sound as if you are conducting an inquisition, but rather to present yourself as being concerned and interested, but needing more information" (80). Where are the performance gaps evidenced within our data? How can we close the identified gaps? What resources will be needed to better position our students for success in the future? How can parents and/or our community help us attain excellence in our academic program? Of course, these are examples of probing questions that may, or may not, fit the discussion that needs to be undertaken on a campus.

The important thing is that the principal is gathering not only performance data evidence but also perceived needs elicited from stakeholders interdependently related by the school improvement process. The critical issue is that the leader is listening to all members of the learning community.

Once these voices are heard, those charged with the planning process need to examine the campus's identified needs and map out goal priorities. Although many methods are available, prioritizing three levels of ranking your goals can be utilized for this planning step.

Envision a target like the one shown in figure 7.2 as an aid in separating the goals into three levels of importance. At the center are the precedence goals that predictably will have the most impact on student success and are supported by the available data evidence indicating the placement of these goals at the center of the school's continuous improvement process. The middle ring of the target represents secondary matters that are valued and deemed worthwhile but are secondary to those goals central to advancing the school's improvement agenda. Last is an outer ring of goals that can be assigned as having marginal impact for improving the delivery of high-quality, student-centered educational opportunity.

Precedence Goals

Precedence goals are, obviously, those the leadership team and internal and external stakeholders view as the most important work needing to be done

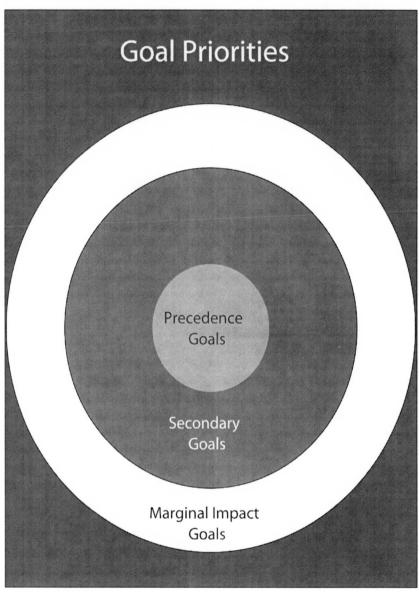

Figure 7.2.   Targeting of Goals

during the year. These are the goals that are essential for continuous academic improvement for all students. They reflect the values and beliefs that are central to the school's mission and call attention to the needs identified through data and by listening to stakeholders. These goals center on matters such as strengthening the school's academic programs, professional development of teachers, creating a technology-rich learning environment, and making connections with parents and the community.

Secondary Goals

Secondary goals are matters that are worthwhile but will not provide maximum "bang for the buck" in improving the instructional program nor to the accomplishment of vision. They are not, nor should they be allowed to become, the most important tasks on which the school is focused.

The inherent requirements of our complex work environment require us to set goals for concerns such as safety, traffic control, extracurricular events, and building and grounds maintenance, all of which are necessary but do not rise to the level of being precedence goals for accomplishing the genuine school improvement work.

Marginal Impact Goals

Finally, there are goals that we know will have minimal impact but acknowledge they routinely have to be accomplished in any organizational environment. These are the day-to-day tasks that may seem important but when juxtaposed with the higher ranking precedence goals seem trivial. Examples might be filing, organizing the textbook room, faculty parking, or creating a master key system for the school. These all may need to be accomplished but can be time bandits ready to rob the instructional team of valuable time for instructional improvement. Many of these marginal impact goals can be delegated or you might find they do not need to be done at all.

Turning Goals into Action

Goal setting will lead to frustration among the school's staff and stakeholders unless they are coupled with logical, systematic action steps. A comprehensive planning process should move from the more abstract long-range goals to more concrete short-term goals with associated goal indicators, strategies, individuals (groups) responsible, reasonable time expectations, and link all of this to available resources both within the formal budget as well as other sources of financial and/or in-kind support.

Short-term goals answer the question, "What do we want to accomplish in the coming year?" Goal indicators are formative subsets of the short-term goals and answer the question, "How will we know we are making progress toward achieving the short-term goals we have set?"

Responsibilities need to be assigned for each goal and its accompanying goal indicators. Individual or group responsibility for short-term goals answers the question, "Who will be accountable for facilitating the accomplishment of this goal?" It is recommended that the leader utilize a system like the one described in chapter 3 (table 3.1) for delegating responsibility by indicating individuals or groups with primary responsibility (P), secondary responsibility (S), and assistance (A).

The campus goal setting process requires a date certain for both the benchmark reporting of progress being made as well as the time target for its accomplishment. This could be expressed by a calendar date or more generally as weekly, monthly, end of grading periods, benchmark dates, semesters, or academic year. The most important issues are that there is a reporting system that communicates progress to relevant stakeholders and that, through the monitoring function, adjustments can be made as situations change. Remember, school improvement is not a linear process even though we have schedules and reporting dates assigned to the goals.

The final goal setting element is to link the school's goals to the budget. Many schools fail to do this effectively due to the goal setting process being on a different timeline from the budgeting process. Setting goals after the budget is adopted makes little, if any, sense.

To accomplish this planning step consider using a simplified cost-benefit, or pro versus con, approach. A cost-benefit analysis provides decision makers with a balanced approach concerning the cost and benefits, or value, inherent in a program or stratagem. When compared against each other the relative merits for the implementation of the approach and its estimated impact on students as well as the campus budget can be predicted.

Modeling this process will require the following steps while considering a strategy's inclusion as a budget request:

1. Describe the strategy (program, instructional approach, etc.).
2. What information do you have about its merits (scientifically based data evidence)?
3. List the positive aspects (student outcomes, program outcomes, staff outcomes, etc.).
4. List the negative aspects (financial resources, human resources, time, etc.).
5. How will implementation of the solution strategy meet the school's vision and specified goals?

Throughout the planning process the leadership team must keep the heart of their decisions on a "what's best for kids" philosophy.

Using Goal Setting as a Motivational Means

As I have visited with colleagues over the years and talked about the organizational and personal benefits of effective goal setting I often hear comments like, "I know how to set goals. I just don't know how to motivate myself or others to accomplish what we know we need to do." Truthfully, inherent in this plea is the single biggest problem we all face with regards to goals—goal attainment. We know *how* to set goals for ourselves and our school but we struggle with the motivation piece needed for goal attainment.

In reality, few of us stay motivated the way we would like whether it is with our exercise regimen, attempts at dieting, or even as this writer has learned, with personal goals like this book project. As a busy school leader, the challenge is to not only be motivated to accomplish personal goals but also how to keep our staff and stakeholders motivated toward the accomplishment of organizational goals.

Keeping the school committed to the follow-through of our goal setting planning requires the leadership team to closely monitor the agreed upon strategies and actions. As they say, "The best-laid plans go awry" and especially at the implementation stage. Tracking your progress is important but keeping the human resources element of your school motivated must be a priority. The principal and leadership team have to become the champions for the school's vision, mission, and goals and serve as cheerleaders for unifying all stakeholders and moving them toward goal attainment.

Developing a positive climate and maintaining direction toward the achievement of campus goals requires building and nurturing relationships as the point of Covey, Merrill, and Merrill's (1994) garden analogy affirms,

Most of us think it would be great if we could just put our gardens—or our lives—on automatic and somehow get the quality-of-life results that come from careful, consistent nurturing of the things that create it.

But life doesn't work that way. We can't just toss out a few seeds, go ahead and do whatever we want to do and expect to come back to find a beautiful, well-groomed garden ready to drop a bountiful harvest of beans, corn, potatoes, carrots, and peas into our basket. We have to water, cultivate, and weed on a regular basis if we are going to enjoy the harvest.

Our lives will bring forth anyway. Things will grow. But the difference between our own active involvement as gardeners and neglect is the difference between a beautiful garden and a weed patch. (77)

As the organizational gardeners, principals and their leadership team need to energize the school's work effort toward the accomplishment of the harvest of success.

When we consider our important responsibility for achieving our school's goals, one thing is certain, leaders who can motivate others to do more than they thought they could will be successful. Miner (2005), in discussing Bernard Bass's (1985) transformational leadership theory, reported that a leader could structure success by encouraging all stakeholders to (1) raise their level of awareness about the importance of the work to be done, for valuing desired outcomes, and always stretching to reach the campus goals; (2) by persuading them to go beyond their own self-interest and replace it with a "what's best for kids" way of thinking; and (3) by altering their need level or expanding their range of needs and wants (363). All three interrelated and interconnected aspects for motivating others to action are necessary for school leaders to accomplish their vision.

Raising the Level of Awareness
We began the discussion of goal setting by basing the process on the values and beliefs held by the organization. We return to this gold standard now as we seek to keep our collective "eyes on the prize" of student academic success and equity. Individuals who have a learner-centered vision for what can, and should, be done to effect this end state will emerge as leaders on the campus. It might stem from the actions of the distributed Value Added Unified Leadership Team or from other individuals who may emerge in nontraditional ways and lead from the side without being a formal leader in the school. In either case the promotion of the school's continuous improvement cause has to be personified by the actions of the principal.

School leaders should be at the forefront in communicating the school's current state and where the school wants to be in the future. Additionally, they must also clearly understand how the school intends to reach their goals and what data evidence will be utilized to gauge progress. Communication of the school's progress has to be presented continuously to internal and external stakeholders in every conceivable forum and format. This should be looked upon as a major responsibility of the principal as a highly visible spokesperson for the school.

But two cautions need to be considered in the communication process. First, reporting of progress and results must be balanced. Communicating the news about a school's academic performance is much less painful when the data is positive than when it is not. Educators must use a balanced approach when reporting to stakeholders. By providing an accurate picture of the school's progress and not an image that has been sanitized for the public, the principal will project an image of being transparent and truthful.

Unfortunately, this is not always the case. A trained gemologist can easily detect a cubic zirconia from a diamond. Too often, in today's educational arena we find artificial leaders more interested in the advancement of their own agenda or career than with transparency when it comes to providing an honest report of progress. Too often we witness district spokespersons, who are highly trained spin doctors, telling the public a cleansed version of what is going on in their schools and sweeping their shortcomings under the proverbial rug.

The old adage attributed to Abraham Lincoln, that you can fool some of the people all of the time, and all of the people some of the time, but you cannot fool all of the people all of the time, rings truthful when it comes to spinning rather than honestly reporting the school's progress.

People in the school organization are just as talented as the gemologist and know whether the leader is providing accurate and full disclosure of all of the data. A true leader is one who can be trusted to give stakeholders the good, the bad, and even, at times, the ugly. Raising stakeholder level of awareness about the importance of the work to be done and, at the same time, owning the problematical outcomes will communicate the school's earnest commitment to reach the goals they have set.

Moving from Self-Directed Interest to Student-Directed Interest

Genuine leaders are committed to providing equitable student-centered learning opportunities for all students under their charge. These leaders are recognized for being risk takers who put students first and resist structuring and operating schools for the satisfaction of the adults in the building.

Leading the school culture from adult-centered to student-centered can be challenging waters to navigate for even the most astute and savvy school leader. The leader's influence over the culture of the campus requires an understanding of the demands and constraints inherent in the principalship and a strong, yet adaptive style.

Yukl (2008) found these implications to include an ability to diagnose situations quickly and couple a response to behaviors that would produce a positive resolution. The adaptive leader must be proficient in the use of a "wide range of behaviors" and, according to Yukl, be proactive when influencing the situation and choosing a behavior (3). Creating a school that both enriches educational opportunities for the students and also results in a better place for the teachers and staff to work takes this type of flexibility and common sense.

To provide an ideal work environment focused on diagnosing and responding to the individual needs of each child requires an understanding of worker autonomy, professional development, and working as a unified team. These productivity concepts have great application for schools and their leadership as expressed and expanded by Haasen and Shea (1997):

- People need full control and autonomy at work. The job has to be their responsibility, and they must be able to make all the important decisions related to their work. At the same time the role of management becomes one of coordinating, being available as a resource of experience and support, and serving as coaches and mentors.
- People need opportunities to learn and to master new knowledge and skills. Successful learning in itself becomes a source of motivation and builds self-esteem. In addition, learning makes people more flexible and lets them understand the interrelationships of a business (i.e., the dependence of each segment of an operation on the others). They must know enough about the enterprise to detect problems, understand the total system affecting those problems, and be able to contribute their ideas, insights, and experience in solving those problems.
- People need to be part of a work team that gives them a base of support and allows them to find their own level of challenge. Work teams make it possible to assign meaningful work segments to a group of people and broaden their responsibilities. This, in turn, makes work more enjoyable. (93)

Bottom line: we all have to become contributing members of the school's learning community and be allowed the flexibility to diagnose and solve challenges in an ever-evolving, student-centered environment.

Elevating Stakeholder Wants and Needs
It has been said that ownership of schools is held by the communities they serve. It is "their schools, their money, and their kids" and as educators we need to acknowledge that we serve the community through our work with their children. The community exerts pressure in varying degrees from the negotiated beliefs ingrained in the vision, to accountability for results, to providing or withholding of needed resources. Rarely are school leaders dealing with a single unified community.

Rather, the school is more likely to serve a complex network of communities that at times join hands and on other issues may be extremely polarized. Schools, and as a result the principal, need to keep their fingers on the pulse of their collective community and especially their power actors.

School support, even when it is at a low level or when polarized, will either drive needed reforms or cause initiatives to die on the vine. A skilled and sensitive principal can craft the needed support and change expectations with a commitment to understanding the community and being responsive to its aspirations. It is through a collaborative approach and the principal's listening and learning from stakeholders that alliances are born that can effect needed change. As Ubben, Hughes, and Norris (2001) state,

> Good instructional leaders are able to harness the interests of the community, taking advantage of the strengths while at the same time focusing on its needs. Over time, an effective instructional leader will even mold the community's expectations for the school, changing satisfaction with mediocrity or special interests to expectations for excellence in the entire program. (42)

Using commonly developed school goals as leverage points for change will support the attainment of the leader's vision for a high-quality, high-performing school.

Chapter Reflection

In the Preflection to this chapter we met veteran principal Cynthia Ann Teasdale with start-of-school blues. She, as most well-intentioned leaders in complex organizations, was having difficulty finding a balance between the seemingly urgent beginning of school tasks and the important issues in both her personal and professional life. Consider the following questions based on the chapter and how Ms. Teasdale represents many of us who confuse what is urgent with what is really important as we search for balance in our careers and personal life.

1. Is it possible that what we see as urgent issues in our day-to-day lives get in the way of what is really important? Why or why not?
2. How could Cynthia Ann Teasdale structure her campus goal setting process to create a high-performance culture and, at the same time, allow more time for herself in her personal life?

3. As a school leader, how could you leverage community support through the goal setting process?
4. Why do schools sometimes fall victim to their focus being more about the adults rather than the kids? How should you work to overcome this crucial dilemma?

~

CHAPTER EIGHT

Reflective Practice

Key #7—Understanding that reflection is a key to continued renewal of the VAULT.

Preflection

Abraham "Abe" Meir lay awake reflecting on the day's events at Provincial Middle School. Being the principal and, presumably, the instructional leader of the school Abe recounted the things that went well and those that had not. Invariably when he took time to reflect his mind seemed to dwell on the latter, those things that needed to be fixed.

This day's reflections were no different for Abe Meir. Having risen through the ranks of a large suburban school district, his instincts for continuous improvement were matchless. He understood that his role as an instructional leader included his support for educator self-directedness for decisions related to instruction and assessment on his campus. A big part of this was the analysis of data and utilizing the information for bridging gaps among student subpopulations.

Abe Meir hated the term *subpopulation* and resisted even using it but it seemed to be ingrained in the school improvement vernacular. While he was at it he mused that he also hated the term *best practices*. The connotation seemed to be rather exclusive of other approaches and limit innovation. But, alas, this was not the elephant in the room.

As he began to focus on the things that needed his attention the most as an instructional leader, the persistent and perplexing challenge of motivating teachers to join him in reflecting on the state's high-stakes student accountability data. He preached to his staff the importance of looking at the available data, understanding what it is telling them, learning from it, and creating action plans for addressing any shortcomings revealed in the data.

It was this last step that had created significant resistance from his staff. He had required his teachers to create Individualized Learning Maps (ILPs) for each student based on the individual student data available. These plans were intended to make sure all students were performing on or above grade level and ensure that no student would fall through the cracks. ILPs had, instead, become an Individualized Learning mess that was challenging his ability to lead effectively. Teachers were quietly revolting and he knew it was only a matter of time before their ire reached the ears of the district's school board.

Abe Meir quietly picked up the phone and called the superintendent of schools. A valued and trusted professional colleague and friend, Dalton Hicks had fought many battles in the Santa Elena district and could be counted on for wise counsel. Abe had always kept the superintendent in the loop concerning the changes he was attempting on his campus, but this was the biggest setback he had faced as a school leader.

Dr. Dalton Hicks greeted Abe Meir with his usual aplomb and cheerfulness. He realized his friend was struggling with a significant challenge to his authority, but this was not Dalton Hicks's first rodeo. Encouragingly, the superintendent said, "You know, Abe, I am reminded of what I remember reading that John Dewey said, something along the order of reflection including looking back and looking forward at an issue. Let's start at the beginning, reflect with me how you approached the implementation of the Individualized Learning Maps.

Abe Meir felt better immediately. His problem was not solved but he had confidence that the reflection process initiated by Dr. Hicks would lead to the identification of alternative solutions. As in the past, he knew he would be trusted to choose the right option and be supported as he and his campus moved forward.

Rigor, Relevance, and Reflection

Reflecting on my personal experience as a young school administrator, I vividly recall the dynamics of serving three masters. Placed in a newly created assistant principal position in the mid-1980s precipitated by the novel concept that school leaders needed to look in classrooms, I rotated among three schools each day freeing the principals to be "highly visible" on their campuses. One campus was a PK–1 early childhood school where I spent half of each day. The other two schools, with grade configurations dictated by a significant lack of facilities in the district, were a second–third grade campus and a fourth–fifth grade campus where I spent two hours each day.

I only mention this walk down memory lane because of what I was able to take from this experience: an understanding that a leader's beliefs and expectations about teaching are critical for school success and that it was seminal to the person I became as a school leader. In my experience working for these three principals only one embodied educational values and beliefs I considered worthy of emulation.

This educator put students first and held sacred a covenant with parents that all students would be successful. Her unambiguous communication of this nonnegotiable belief system was grounded in a deep-seated wisdom that realized improved educational opportunity occurred campus by campus and classroom by classroom. The key to school improvement for this principal was simply to attract and employ a nurturing teacher for every classroom.

It was not enough for teachers on her campus to "love children," they had to know their content and "know what to do" to ensure academic success and equity for *all* students. Although I learned from the other two principals—mostly subpoenal obedience, it was her understanding of the importance of true professionalism in the classroom—what I now recognize to be democratic and reflective practice—that served as an exemplar for my future conduct as a campus and district leader.

Few would argue that schools in the twenty-first century have become very complex and challenging to manage. Day (2000) affirms this trend, stating, "School principals' work, like that of teachers, has intensified and become more complex in recent times" (113). The composite of additional role responsibilities coupled with increased expectations places a tremendous burden on the principal for achieving the vision of high-quality and equitable educational opportunities.

The fast-paced and acknowledged complexity accompanying the principal practitioner's practice often forestalls ongoing reflective assessment of his or her decision making. Often what substitutes for quality decision making is a "trust my gut" instinct-driven reaction to on-the-job challenges. Results from this approach tend to be minimally effective at best and, at worst, serve to create an educationally toxic leadership culture. Principals of this ilk become increasingly isolated from their learning community colleagues and create organizational frustration with the wisdom and credibility of the leaders' decisions and actions.

Visionary principals who create rigorous and relevant conditions that support and develop others, problem solve by asking pertinent questions about practice, and accept their role as lead learner are able to reflect on what can, and should, be done to facilitate high expectations among all stakeholders. This requires the principal's creation of conditions for reflection where all stakeholders are invited to reflect on the school's instructional practice.

In order to create the conditions supportive of reflection three attendant issues that impact success must be considered: (1) the facilitation of reflection, including how to engage the community of learners in meaningful reflection and dialogue; (2) the appropriate setting for reflection, including reserving times and places for reflection; and (3) reflection-driven catalytic action steps, including the fine-tuning of the school's goal attainment strategies and assessment indicators that continue to distill the school's improvement progress. The principal's success in the engagement of others as a community of reflective practitioners has to be focused on these steps for continued success.

Facilitating Reflection

School leaders wishing to develop reflective practice must first be recognized for being not only an organization change agent but also a change agent of self and others. Unquestionably, the leader must be willing to recognize how to change the organization while, at the same time, being open to changing his or her own practice.

Great leaders understand the importance of engaging others in reflective practice and empowering them to serve as problem solvers. Razik and Swanson (2010) find distributed leadership to be a requisite in the new millennium involving "multiple leaders who engage in shared or collaborative leadership" (99). Developing and engaging others in reflection on critical issues facing the school organization not only enhances the leadership alliance, it also promotes rigor and relevance.

John Dewey has often been cited for his encouragement of reflective practice and is still looked to today when leader-practitioners seek to distill the criteria for his notions concerning reflection. Rogers (2002) extracted the following characteristics and underpinnings of reflection from the works of Dewey in an effort to better define its significance to practice:

1. Reflection is a meaning-making process that moves a learner from one experience into the next with deeper understanding of its relationships with and connections to other experiences and ideas. It is the thread that makes continuity of learning possible, and ensures the progress

of the individual and, ultimately, society. It is a means to essentially moral ends.

2. Reflection is a systematic, rigorous, disciplined way of thinking with its roots in scientific inquiry.
3. Reflection needs to happen in community, in interaction with others.
4. Reflection requires attitudes that value the personal and intellectual growth of oneself and of others. (845)

Each of these attributes of reflective practice should resonate with school leaders desiring to make a significant impact with their community of learners. These characteristics should serve as the school improvement building blocks for continuous improvement of the school.

Visionary leaders comfortable with sharing power rely heavily on the impact gained through effective interpersonal, intrapersonal, and group interactions to create the culture necessary for systematic, rigorous discourse. Bringing an often diverse group of stakeholders together to reflect and dialogue on school reform issues requires a leader willing to share and differentiate leadership.

While engendering a culture of reflective practice a learning community develops, resulting in sustainable change. The leader's skill at fostering a synergistic culture promotes an inclusive sharing of responsibility for learner-centeredness that, once accepted and widened, will permeate the school and result in improved student success and equity.

In order to facilitate the campus community's dialogue on critical issues the leader must create the conditions for reflective practice that respectfully values all voices. Leadership in this arena involves an understanding of the importance not only of reflective practice, but also of proficiency in interpersonal, intrapersonal, and group communication.

Communicating with others requires the leader to not only verbalize the vision held for the organization but also earnestly listen to the views held by others. Howard Gardner (2004) describes this "interpersonal intelligence" as the ability to understand others and "figure out their motivations, work effectively with them, and, if necessary, manipulate them" (39).

Effective interactions with stakeholders are the heart blood of the school organization and are predicated on the leader's own reflection and capacity to self-diagnose personal communication strengths and weaknesses. A leader's ability to introspectively analyze his or her own motivations is critical for building trusting relationships with organizational others. Gardner (2004) refers to this as "intrapersonal intelligence" where the individual "possesses a good working model of herself; can identify personal feelings, goals, fears, strengths, and weaknesses; and can . . . use that model to make judicious decisions in her life" (39).

Facilitating groups and the importance of how the leader approaches making decisions regarding school improvement matters with the school's internal and external stakeholders can never be underestimated. Decisions can be made along a continuum ranging from directive, as in the case of an emergency, to collaborative where consensus is the desired outcome. Certainly, the latter is desired when a critical instructional change is being considered.

Whenever individuals have to support and implement needed changes, school leaders must be cognizant of their role as the facilitator of group decision making. Individual stakeholders within the school must be brought into the discussion on the strengths and weaknesses of critical issues in a transparent, open, reflective dialogue. Penman (2000) describes this as mutuality where "all participants are committed and able to make some contribution to the process" (92).

It is crucial that these conversations take place within an atmosphere where every voice is respected in order to garner needed support for reforms and avoid the inevitable pitfall of resistance to change that Schutz (1979) calls attention to,

> The question of consensus is central to decision making. In a deeper sense, consensus means that everyone in the group feels that the group understands his position and his feelings about it, and he feels, then, that the group should take a particular course of action even though he does not personally agree. If the individual is not allowed to voice his own feelings and reasons for voting against the particular issue, he will, at least unconsciously, resist the efficient functioning of the group from that point on. (250)

School leaders simply have to become adept at working with groups to effect the changes needed on their campus. As Adler, Rosenfeld, and Proctor (2004) accurately calculate, "Perhaps the most important insight about . . . working groups is that they can make the difference between satisfaction and misery" (369).

Through reflective practice leaders can avoid the misery generated by discontent and disillusionment and create organizational culture where open research-based dialogue is valued. Cunningham and Cordeiro (2003) support this, stating, "Reflective practice means staying abreast of the latest research in practice, researching your own practice, experimenting with new approaches, reflecting on your own practice, and sharing your insights" (168).

Reflection that informs practice can be either spontaneous or planned and leaders must capitalize on opportunities to cultivate these prospective experiences in their own practice as well as with others. Whether it is the informal reflective introspection resulting from a professional challenge, the proverbial "teachable moment" when the leader has the opportunity to foster the professional growth of others, or a well-planned and articulated school improvement conversation, an environment conducive to the open exchange of ideas must be created.

With the incredibly busy professional and personal schedules in the new millennium where change is a constant and finding time to reflect a luxury, leaders must make reflective practice a priority. Barnett and O'Mahony (2006) strengthen this view, stating, "Becoming more reflective about their practice is an important way for educational leaders to reveal their assumptions and to make better informed decisions" (499). By modeling reflection leaders communicate to stakeholders their ability to utilize multiple sources of data in making informed decisions.

But reflective practice cannot be limited to the leader alone. Day (2000) posits, "Others are necessary at some points in the process. Peer partnerships and networks—discussions and dialogues between practitioners with common purposes—are needed to move from routine to reflective practice in schools" (123). Where other contributors can critique schoolwide practice and professional growth is encouraged, true learning communities emerge.

School improvement flourishes when leaders create a reflective atmosphere based on shared values and beliefs and focused on the school's teaching-learning process. Barnett and O'Mahony (2006) encourage leaders to adopt a "mental model of reflection" guided by the prompts "What? So what? Now what?" to guide them in building schoolwide reflection concerning school improvement initiatives relative to their own practice (519).

Moving from Reflection to Action
Moving from reflective dialogue to "Now what?" requires catalytic actions that are planned, implemented, and assessed. To reflect on school improvement issues is important but turning those ideas into relevant and rigorous practice is yet another challenge. This requires true leadership and a leader's commitment to a continuing communication with those stakeholders with a vested interest.

The reader is encouraged to consider the strategies outlined in previous chapters to begin working with others to advance your learning community toward the attainment of instructional goals. Envisioning the accomplishment of democratic principles based on commonly held values and beliefs will thus become a self-fulfilling prophesy that will VAULT your school to success!

Chapter Reflection

1. As a school principal leading change on your campus, how would you encourage reflective practice among stakeholders?
2. How will you facilitate your own reflection and that of others and use the results for catalytic action?
3. What advice would you give to Abe Meir regarding reflective practice?

References

Adler, R. B., Rosenfeld, L. B., & Proctor II, R. F. (2004). *Interplay: The process of interpersonal communication*. New York: Oxford University Press.

Barker, J. (n.d.). *Discovering the Future Series: The power of vision*. Star Thrower.

Barnett, B. G. & O'Mahony, G. R. (2006). Developing a culture of reflection: Implications for school improvement. *Reflective Practice*, vol. 7, no. 4.

Bluedorn, A. C. & Ferris, S. P. (2004). Temporal depth, age, and organizational performance. In C. Fuchs Epstein & A. L. Kalleberg (Eds.), *Fighting for time: Shifting boundaries of work and social life*. New York: Russell Sage Foundation.

Bolman, L. G. & Deal, T. E. (2003). Reframing organizations: Artistry, choice, and leadership. San Francisco, CA: Jossey-Bass.

Boreen, J. & Niday, D. (2003). *Mentoring beyond boundaries: Helping beginning teachers succeed in challenging situations*. Portland, ME: Stenhouse.

Burka, J. B. (1983). *Procrastination: Why you do it, what to do about it*. Reading, MA: Addison-Wesley.

Camburn, E., Rowan, B., & Taylor, J. (n.d.). *Distributed leadership in schools: The case of elementary schools adopting comprehensive school reform models*. Consortium for Policy Research in Education. Retrieved June 18, 2009, from www.sii.soe.umich.edu/documents/EEPA%20Dist%20Leadership%20Revision%202%20V1.pdf.

Chambers, H. E. (2004). *My way or the highway: The micromanagement survival guide*. San Francisco, CA: Berrett-Koehler Publishers.

Combs, A..W. (1988). New assumptions for educational reform. In P. C. Duttweiler, *Organizing for excellence* (pp. 18–19). Austin, TX: Southwest Educational Development Laboratory.

Corcoran, T. B. (1995). *Helping teachers teach well: Transforming professional development*. Consortium for Policy Research in Education. New Brunswick, NJ.

Retrieved May 26, 2009, from eric.ed.gov/ERICDocs/data/ericdocs2sql/content_ storage_01/0000019b/80/14/3c/24.pdf.

Covey, S. (1999). *Living the 7 habits: The courage to change.* New York: Fireside.

———. (2004). *The 8th habit: From effectiveness to greatness.* New York: Free Press.

Covey, S. R., Merrill, A. R., & Merrill, R. R. (1994). *First things first: To live, to love, to learn, to leave a legacy.* New York: Simon & Schuster.

Cunningham, W. C. & Cordeiro, P. A. (2003). *Educational leadership: A problem-based approach.* Boston: Allyn & Bacon.

———. (2006). *Educational leadership: A problem-based approach.* Boston: Pearson.

———. (2009). *Educational leadership: A bridge to improved practice.* Boston: Pearson.

Dana Center. (2004). *Gap analysis: Overview of identifying gaps process.* Austin, TX: Charles A. Dana Center. Retrieved July 30, 2009, from www.utdanacenter.org/ downloads/presentations/gapanalysis_march04.pdf.

Darling-Hammond, L. & McLaughlin, M. W. (1995). Policies that support professional development in an era of reform. *Phi Delta Kappan,* vol. 76.

Day, C. (2000). Effective leadership and reflective practice. *Reflective Practice,* vol. 1, no. 1.

Deal, T. E. & Peterson, K. D. (2007). Eight roles of symbolic leaders. In *The Jossey-Bass Reader on Educational Leadership,* 2nd ed. San Francisco: John Wiley & Sons.

Dewey, J. (1938/1972). *Experience & education.* New York: The Macmillan Company.

DiPaola, M. F. & Hoy, W. H. (2008). *Principals improving instruction: Supervision, evaluation, and professional development.* Boston: Pearson.

Donaldson Jr., G. A. & Marnik, G. F. (1995). *Becoming better leaders: The challenge of improving student learning.* Thousand Oaks, CA: Corwin Press.

Eckman, E. W. (2007, May). The coprincipalship: It's lonely at the top. *Journal of School Leadership,* vol. 17, no. 3.

Educational Research Service. (2000). *The principal, keystone of a high-achieving school: Attracting and keeping the leaders we need.* Arlington, VA: Educational Research Service.

Eichinger, R. W. & Lombardo, M. M. (2001–2003). *Success profile: School principal.* Developed for Lominger Limited. Retrieved July 23, 2009, from www.microsoft .com/education/competencies/successprofile_principal.mspx.

Farber, S. (2004). *The radical leap.* Chicago: Dearborn Trade Publishing.

Fitzpatrick, K. A. (2002). *Indicators of school quality.* Schaumburg, IL: National Study of School Evaluation.

Fullan, M. G. (1995). The limits and the potential of professional development. In T. R. Guskey, & M. Huberman (Eds.), *Professional development in education: New paradigms and practices.* New York: Teachers College Press.

———. (2001). *Leading in a culture of change: Being effective in complex times.* San Francisco: Jossey-Bass.

Gardner, H. (2004). *Changing minds: The art and science of changing our own and other people's minds.* Boston: Harvard Business School Press.

Gleeson, K. (1998). *The high-tech personal efficiency program*. New York: John Wiley & Sons.

Gopalakrishnan, S. & Hill, B. (2009). Designing for organizational transformation: Key ideas in creating a coherent, continuously emerging system. *Ball Foundation Review*, vol. 9, no. 1 (Spring). Retrieved July 24, 2009, from www.ballfoundation .org/ei/resources/review/Review_Spring_2009.pdf.

Gutherie, J. W. & Schuermann, P. J. (2010). *Successful school leadership*. Boston: Allyn & Bacon.

Haasen, A. & Shea, G. F. (1997). *A better place to work*. New York: AMA Membership Publications Division.

Harris, A. (2002, September). *Distributed leadership in schools; Leading or misleading?* Paper presented at the British Educational Leadership Management & Administration Conference. Birmingham, England. Retrieved June 19, 2009, from eric .ed.gov/ERICDocs/data/ericdocs2sql/content_storage_01/0000019b/80/1b/83/95 .pdf.

Henderson, J. G. (1999). The journey of democratic curriculum leadership: An overview. In J. G. Henderson & K. R. Kesson, *Understanding democratic curriculum leadership*. New York: Teachers College Press.

Hochheiser, R. M. (1998). *Time management*. Hauppauge, NY: Barron's.

Hoy, A. L. & Hoy, W. K. (2009). *Instructional leadership: A Research-based guide to learning in schools*. Boston: Pearson.

Hoy, W. K. & Tarter, C. J. (1995). *Administrators solving the problems of practice: Decision-making concepts, cases, and consequences*. Boston: Allyn and Bacon.

Interstate School Leaders Licensure Consortium (ISLLC). (1996). *Standards for school leaders*. Washington, DC: Council of Chief State School Officers.

Jenlink, P. M., Ed. (2009). Dewey's democracy and education revisited. Lanham, MD: Rowman & Littlefield Education.

Keefe, J. W. & Jenkins, J. M. (1997). *Instruction and the learning environment*. Larchmont, NY: Eye On Education.

Kelly, C. & Peterson, K. D. (2007). *The work of principals and their preparation: Addressing critical needs for the twenty-first century*. In *The Jossey-Bass Reader on Educational Leadership*, 2nd ed. San Francisco: John Wiley & Sons.

Kincheloe, J. L. (1999). Critical democracy and education. In J. G. Henderson & K. R. Kesson, *Understanding democratic curriculum leadership*. New York: Teachers College Press.

———. (2005). Foreword. In M. Gordon (2005), *Ten common myths in American education*. Brandon, VT: Holistic Education Press. Retrieved August 29, 2005, from great-ideas.org/Gordon_pages.pdf.

Kotter, J. P. (1998). *What leaders really do*. Harvard Business Review on Leadership. Boston: Harvard Leadership Review Paperback.

Levine, A. (2005). *Educating school leaders*. Washington, DC: The Education Schools Project.

Lezotte, L. W. (1991). *Correlates of effective schools: The first and second generation.* Okemos, MI: Effective Schools Products.

Lezotte, L. W. & Pepperl, J. C. (1999). *The effective schools process: A proven path to learning for all.* Okemos, MI: Effective Schools Products.

Mackenzie, R. A. (1997). *The time trap.* New York: Amacom.

Malone, R. J. (2001). Principal mentoring. *ERIC Digest* 149 (July).

Manz, C. C. & Sims, Jr., H. P. (1992). Becoming a superleader. In R. Glaser. & C. Bayley (Eds.), *Classic readings in self-managing teamwork.* King of Prussia, PA: Organization Design and Development.

Mayrowertz, D. (2008). Making sense of distributed leadership: Exploring the multiple usages of the concept in the field. *Education Administration Quarterly,* vol. 44, no. 424. Retrieved June 17, 2009, from eaq.sagepub.com/cgi/content/abstract/44/3/424.

Miner, J. B. (2005). *Organizational behavior 1: Essential theories of motivation and leadership.* Armonk, NY: M. E. Sharpe.

Murphy, J., Elliott, S., Goldring, E., & Porter, A. (2007, April). Leadership for learning: A research-based model and taxonomy of behaviors. *School Leadership & Management,* vol. 27, no. 2, 179–201. Retrieved June 18, 2009, from doi:10.1080/13632430701237420.

No Child Left Behind Act (NCLB). (2001). *Public Law 107-110 Title II, Subpart 1, Sec 2113 (c) 1 (a) (ii).* Washington, DC.

Oncken, Jr., W. & Wass, D. L. (1974, November/1999, December). Management time: Who's got the monkey? *Harvard Business Review.* Retrieved June 18, 2009, from www.kingfahdweb.com/library/self-develop/monkey.pdf.

Penman, R. (2000). *Reconstructing communicating: Looking to a future.* Mahwah, NJ: Lawrence Erlbaum Associates.

Peters, T. (1997). *The circle of innovation.* New York: Alfred A. Knopf.

Porter, A. C., Garet, M. S., Desimone, L., Yoon, K. S., & Birman, B. F. (2000, October). *Does professional development change teaching practice? Results from a three year study.* Jessup, MD: ED Pubs. Retrieved June 21, 2006, from www.ed.gov/rschstat/eval/teaching/epdp/report.doc.

Pratt, S. (2002). *Native pragmatism: Rethinking the roots of American philosophy.* Bloomington, IN: Indiana University Press. Retrieved February 26, 2005, from iupress.indiana.edu/textnet/0-253-34078-0/025310890X.htm.

Putnam, R. D. (2000). *Bowling alone: The collapse and revival of the American community.* New York: Simon & Schuster.

Razik, T. A. & Swanson, A. D. (2010). *Fundamental concepts of educational leadership and management.* Boston: Allyn & Bacon.

Richert, A. E., Stoddard, P., & Kass, M. (2001). *The promise of partnership for promoting reform.* In F. O. Rust & H. Freidus (Eds.), *Guiding school change: The role and work of change agents.* New York: Teachers College Press.

Rogers, C. (2002, June). Defining reflection: Another look at John Dewey and reflective thinking. *Teachers College Record,* vol. 104, no. 4.

2

Rowley, J. B. (1999, May). The good mentor. *Educational Leadership*, vol. 56, no. 3, 20.

Rust, F. O. & Freidus, H. (Eds.). (2001). *Guiding school change: The role and work of change agents*. New York: Teachers College Press.

Samier, E. (2000). Public administration mentorship: Conceptual and pragmatic considerations. *Journal of Educational Administration*, vol. 38, no. 1, 83–101.

Schutz, W. C. (1979). The interpersonal underworld. In *Harvard Business Review on Human Relations*. New York: Harper & Row.

Scott, D. (1980). *How to put more time in your life*. Crawfordsville, IN: R. R. Donnelley & Sons.

Sergiovanni, T. J. (2006). *The principalship: A reflective practice perspective*. Boston: Pearson.

———. (2009). *The principalship: A reflective practice perspective*. Boston: Pearson.

Shahid, B., Chavez, R., Hall, B., Long, S., Pritchard, A., Randolph, B., Sullivan, J., & Wildman, L. (2001). How can principals spend more time on instructional leadership? *Education*, vol. 121, no. 3 (Spring), 506. Retrieved June 18, 2009, from Professional Development Collection database.

Shaver, H. (2004). *Organize, communicate, empower! How principals can make time for leadership*. Thousand Oaks, CA: Corwin Press.

Southern Regional Education Board (SREB, n.d.). *Schools can't wait: Accelerating the redesign of university principal preparation programs*. Atlanta, GA: Southern Regional Education Board.

Stanford, B. (1998). *Charting school change: Improving the odds for successful school reform*. Thousand Oaks, CA: Corwin Press.

Starratt, (1995). *Leaders with vision: The quest for school renewal*. Thousand Oaks, CA: Corwin Press.

Stufflebeam, D. L. (2002, June). *CIPP evaluation model checklist*. Retrieved July 29, 2009, from www.wmich.edu/evalctr/checklists/cippchecklist.htm.

Thornton, P. B. (1999). *Be the leader: Make the difference*. Torrance, CA: Griffin Publishing Group.

Ubben, G. C., Hughes, L. W., & Norris, C. J. (2001). *The principal: Creative leadership for effective schools*. Boston: Allyn and Bacon.

U.S. Department of Education. (2001). No Child Left Behind Act of 2001. Retrieved July 9, 2009, from www.ed.gov/policy/elsec/leg/esea02/index.html.

Webster's New Twentieth Century Dictionary. (1955). Cleveland, OH: The World Publishing Company.

Wong, S. L. (2001). *Managing diversity: Institutions and the politics of educational change*. Lanham, MD: Rowman & Littlefield Publishers, Inc.

Young, C. Y. & Wright, J. V. (2001). Mentoring: The component for success. *Journal of Instructional Psychology*, vol. 28, no. 3, 203.

Yukl, G. (2008). The importance of flexible leadership. In R. B. Kaiser (chair), *The Importance and Development of Flexible Leadership*, practitioner forum. San Francisco: 23rd annual conference of the Society for Industrial-Organizational

Psychology, April 2008. Retrieved from www.kaplandevries.com/images/uploads/ Importance_of_FL_SIOP08Yukl.pdf.

Zmuda, A., Kuklis, R. & Kline, E. (2004). *Transforming schools: Creating a culture of continuous improvement*. Alexandria, VA: Association for Supervision and Curriculum Development.

~

About the Author

John C. Leonard is an associate professor at Stephen F. Austin State University. Prior to joining the SFA faculty, he was employed for twenty-nine years as a public school teacher, assistant principal, high school principal, assistant superintendent, and superintendent of schools. Leonard earned a B.A. in music education from Southwest Texas State University, an M.S. in music education from the University of Illinois, and a doctorate in educational leadership from Texas A&M University, College Station. Leonard teaches in the principal and superintendent preparation programs and the educational leadership doctoral program at SFA. His primary areas of interest are organizational management, human resource management, and school-community relations. In 2005, he received the Teaching Excellence Award for the Department of Secondary Education and Educational Leadership. In addition to teaching, Leonard was interim associate dean for the James I. Perkins College of Education with primary responsibilities for its highly successful National Council for the Accreditation of Teacher Education reaccreditation.

Breinigsville, PA USA
01 August 2010
242823BV00001B/3/P